Happiness
is a
HABIT

Happiness
is a HABIT

SIMPLE DAILY RITUALS
that INCREASE ENERGY, IMPROVE WELL-BEING,
and ADD JOY TO EVERY DAY

MICHELE PHILLIPS

PLAIN SIGHT PUBLISHING
AN IMPRINT OF CEDAR FORT, INC.
SPRINGVILLE, UT

Disclaimer:

Please read through all the steps, participate at your own risk, and use good judgment. This book may offer you ideas that may or may not be good for you based on your health and fitness level. These ideas are not meant to take the place of professional advice from your doctor or therapist. Before starting any exercise or diet program, you must get medical clearance.

ISBN 13: 978-1-4621-1257-9

Published by Plain Sight Publishing, an imprint of Cedar Fort, Inc.,
2373 W. 700 S., Springville, UT 84663
Distributed by Cedar Fort, Inc., www.cedarfort.com

Library of Congress Cataloging-in-Publication Data

Phillips, Michele, 1964- author.
Happiness is a habit : simple daily rituals that increase energy, improve well being, and add joy to every day / Michele Phillips.
    pages cm
Includes bibliographical references and index.
ISBN 978-1-4621-1257-9 (alk. paper)
1. Happiness--Psychological aspects. 2. Self-esteem--Psychological aspects. I. Title.

BF575.H27P455 2013
158--dc23

2013033031

Cover design by Angela D. Baxter
Cover design © 2013 by Lyle Mortimer
Edited and typeset by Deborah Spencer

Printed in the United States of America

10 9 8 7 6 5 4 3 2 1

Printed on acid-free paper

This book is dedicated to my family: My mother, Janet; my dad, Domingo; my sister, Darlene; and my brother, Alan. These are the roots of where my happy habits come from. It is through the love, support, and encouragement of my family that I was able to grow and develop into the strong, confident woman I am today. And to my darling Gary, who has entered my life more recently, but who has made everything better. I love and adore you all.

Praise for
Happiness is a Habit

"This book is packed with great advice, based on rigorous, scientific evidence, and communicated in an accessible and engaging manner. Adopting the rituals that Michele Phillips recommends can help you lead a happier, healthier life."

—Tal Ben Shahar, PhD, author of *Happier* and *Being Happy*

"Happiness is a state of being, not a place to arrive at! Michele Phillips shows us how to experience day to day the real happiness that exists already inside each of us."

—Robert Holden, PhD, author of *Happiness NOW* and *Shift Happens!*

"I always thought my life was good. It is! And here comes Michele Phillips, offering 44 simple but powerful habits of happiness along with the prospect of reaching yet another dimension of a fascinating and greatly satisfying overall development: a truly happy life! Thank you, Michele. I love you for that!"

—Udo Fichtner, husband, father, globetrotter, and Global Head of Human Resources, Hirschvogel Automotive Group, Germany

"Michele makes adopting healthy habits so simple, even the biggest couch potato will be inspired to take action! Her book provides foolproof strategies that anyone can use to live a happier and more rewarding life."

—Dawn Miller, PhD, dawnmillernutrition.com

"Michele Phillips's book, *Happiness is a Habit*, is a must-read for anyone who wishes to live their life to the fullest. Michele provides readers with practical steps to make the changes they need to experience real and lasting happiness. I love this book and I read it from cover to cover in one night. Michele is genius!"

—Dr. Lisa Brooks-Greaux, Global Head of Learning & Development, Zoetis

Contents

Acknowledgments

As the saying goes, it takes a village to raise a child, and it has taken a village to get me to this point. So many wonderful people have supported me, believed in me, and listened to me talk about this book for many years. Now the day is here and I am eternally grateful to all of them.

I must start with my parents who have always supported and encouraged me my entire life. Their love and belief in me, along with my grandparents, gave me a solid foundation on which to build. My mother is a woman of quiet strength. She is the rock and the steady, dependable force in our family. She is always cheerful, warm, easy-going, and loving, and she is always there when I need her. Without saying a word, Mom does whatever it takes to keep us all together. My father has an inquisitive mind, tells it like it is, and has the biggest heart I know. When he is happy, everyone knows it, and he spreads his joy everywhere. He has a genuine spirit. My dad has the wonderful gift of being able to articulate what is in his heart and tell the people closest to him how he feels. It is beautiful to see this in action, and I have always admired him for that.

My brother, Alan, always pushes me to see the other side of things even when I don't want to. I often feel he pushes too hard, but at the end of the day, I know that he is the one who has my back. My sister, Darlene, is always there for me at the exact moment I need her, without me having to say a word. Her thoughtful notes, calls, flowers, or words of inspiration are always given at the exact time that I need them most. She may not say it, but she feels my heart in hers.

My former husband, Stephen, is the person who inspired me to try new things, to reach higher, and to raise my standards. He taught me how to leave my comfort zone.

My friend Susann Heller inspires me every day to live with passion just by living her own life. I am in awe of her ability to make simple pleasures spectacular and the effort she puts into bringing beauty to everything. My business associate, mentor, and now friend, Lisa Brooks-Greaux, has been on this journey with me for many years. She encouraged me to go back to school, start my own business, and write this book. For ten years she gently nudged me to tell my story and to own my power. Her guidance and her belief in me helped me to believe in myself. When I mention Lisa, I must also mention Pierre Dobson and Denise Williams. We call ourselves "The Village," and through working with each other for over twenty years we have developed a wonderful bond and support system. Coralie Rogers is the one person who spends the most time with me, as we work together regularly. Coralie has heard it all from me. She has heard me go on and on and on and on, and she has always listened and has given sound advice. We have shared great moments, fun work experiences, and some good belly laughs while traveling. Christine Baker is the angel who navigated me through the book writing process, held me accountable, and laid out a road map for me to follow. Her guidance and advice helped keep me focused and bring this book to life.

Christine, in addition to the good people at Cedar Fort Publishing, have made publishing my first book a wonderful experience. Each person I have dealt with has been kinder and more accommodating than the last.

Last, but by no means least, as they say, my loving and remarkable husband, Gary, who has opened his heart to me in a way that no one has ever done before. He has encouraged and supported me every step of the way, and he has wrapped me up in a love so genuine and utterly beautiful that he makes me feel as if every love song ever written was written especially for me. He is my treasure, and the love that we share is the kind most women dream of. I am so grateful for his precious and special love.

All of these people and many more have supported me, listened to me, advised me, believed in me, and made me feel blessed beyond belief. I love you and am so grateful you are all in my life.

Love & Light,
Michele

Introduction

The world belongs to the energetic.

—Ralph Waldo Emerson

Do you want to be happier? Do you want to experience more joy in your life? Do you want to build a strong foundation for yourself so when life doesn't go as planned you can remain peaceful and strong?

If you answered yes, come along with me. I am going to share with you a number of ideas, practices, laws, or habits (call them what you want), but I guarantee if you are consistent and committed, these habits will change your life as they changed mine.

This book is for people who want to make an investment in themselves. This is NOT an overnight magic pill, a fad, or a quick fix. The habits I will outline in this book take time and discipline. Yet if applied, they will strengthen what I call your core—the depths of your very being. The actual definition of the word "core" is "the central most important part of something."[1] For the purposes of this book, your core is your mental, spiritual, emotional, and physical health—the core of who you are deep within.

I have read countless books over the years with similar messages. Why then should you spend your time reading this one? Herein lies your first challenge. When you read a section of this book and you find yourself saying to yourself, "been there, done that, read the book," that is fine. The next question I want you to ask yourself is, "am I using it?" Just because you know something doesn't mean you use it. For example, smoking causes cancer, and seat belts save lives. If you eat a healthy diet and move around a few times a week, you'll be healthier. While most people wouldn't argue with me on those points, most people don't apply what they know to their lives. The goal of this book is to get you to look at your current habits and start, slowly at first, to build new, better, more powerful habits. I am living proof that it can be done.

The biggest excuse people make to me is that they don't have the time. There are 8,766 hours in a year. I would like to assume that you can carve out some time for yourself, yet over and over again people tell me they don't have time. What I have learned is you don't ever find the time to do many of the things I suggest, but you make the time. You have to ask yourself: why can't you seem to find a few hours for you? In my opinion the quest to improve yourself is worth every ounce of effort.

What are the benefits of a strong core? They are numerous and varied. Suffice it to say that a strong core will improve your overall performance and productivity, improve your health, and give you more energy and happiness. With a strong core you will have the confidence, tools, and strength to get through the tough times in your life. Like a tree with deep roots, or a person with unyielding faith, you will weather the storms of your life. When there are no storms and life is calm, you will soar and glide through your days, finding success, laughter, love, and fulfillment at every turn. It will look to others as if you glide effortlessly and things come easy to you, but you will know the secret. You have taken the time to strengthen your core, build your confidence, and grow your mind. Like an athlete, you have worked hard, put in long hours of your own time for your personal development, and built your spiritual, mental, and physical muscles. And when your core is strong, everyone around you will benefit.

The danger of not having a strong core will result in imbalances: physically, emotionally, mentally, and spiritually. Many people know too well the effects of a weak core. Physically, they suffer with high blood pressure, fatigue, stress, and migraines. Emotionally they experience feelings of depression and feel disconnected from the people in their lives. They live in fear and feel as if they have lost control. Mentally they are drained and suffer from hurried sickness. They display obsessive behavior and entertain ruminating thoughts. Last, they are spiritually broken and disconnected from their own intuition and source.

My goal for you is that you read this book and look for things that resonate with you. That you tune into your own body and intuition. At your core you already have all the answers. My task is simply to lead you back and stoke the flame that burns deep within you. I will take you on a journey back to your true self.

In our current world of achievement and gain, we often move too fast. As a result we lose the essence of who we are. We measure our worth on our output and the opinion of others. We disconnect from our core self in an effort to fulfill the unspoken pressures of society. We give into workaholism and the accumulation of material things. We compromise our own best interests in order to make other people happy. We respond at all hours of the day and night to emails, even while on vacation. We jump when we are told and we never take a "real" day off. When we live our lives this way on a consistent basis, we weaken our core, we become empty and unfulfilled, and this creates more fear and insecurity. Our insecurity and fear of failing leads us to constantly try to prove ourselves, which leads to more hours at work. It becomes a vicious cycle.

On the other hand, if you take the time to strengthen your core, you will find the courage and the strength to speak your mind, ask for what you need, and say no when you have to. You will operate from a place of sincerity, truth, and wisdom. In a world of delete or be deleted, you have to ask yourself what your priorities are and what the cost of living tweet by tweet means to your core self. Just because something is popular does not mean it is worthwhile. We live in a world of distractions that literally "dumb us down"; television and the Internet are filled with mindless, time-consuming addictions. Millions of people waste millions of hours busying themselves with popular mindless distractions. By picking up this book, you have chosen to take the road less traveled; this road may be uncomfortable, challenging at times, and often unpopular. When you take the road less traveled, you may find yourself alone. Your friends may not like the new you and tempt you to take up your old ways, but this is where your strength really counts. Do you go along with the masses, follow the crowd, and go down the same toxic road as them? Or do you choose a different road? I promise you if you stay on this path, new people, new experiences, and new adventures await you.

When you read this book, if something in you stirs and your heart beats a little faster, that excitement is all you need to validate that you are on the right path. Whether our lives are similar or different, I know you have a dream in your heart. I know you have a calling for something you may not be able to name yet. I know there are things about your life you wish were different, or things you may want to improve or change. I know you have areas in your life that you are confident in and areas in your life where you have no confidence at all, or maybe just need improvement. I want to share my journey with you so that you gain belief in yourself and gain the motivation you've been looking for. I want you to look at what I have done and say to yourself, "Me too. If she can do it, so can I." I want you to grow, bloom, and develop the strength to find whatever it is you desire for yourself. I want you to succeed, and I know that together we can get there.

I believe that this book has made it to your hands for a reason. That you know deep inside you can be more and do more. I want you to listen to your own insights and then to take action. I want you to believe in your own dreams, thoughts, and ideas, and remind yourself that within you is everything you need. I want you to know that you always have a choice.

I adopted a saying over ten years ago: MAKE it a great day. I must have heard someone say it and I loved it. The difference between "Have" a great day and "MAKE" it a great day is that it puts the responsibility into your own hands. You decide whether or not to MAKE it a great day. You always have a choice.

1

"We are what we repeatedly do. Excellence, then, is not an act, but a habit."

—Aristotle

Your Life Is Run by Your Habits

It all comes down to your habits. The experts tell us that over 40 percent of what you do every day is based on habits.[1] I would venture to guess that it is a lot higher than that. Your habits are the things you do on automatic pilot: how you respond to events, like drive a car or the way you talk to your spouse. It is your unconscious way of behaving in the world. The gift or the curse of habits is that they require no conscious energy.[2] You perform them without even thinking about it. Some habits feed you and make you stronger, such as a nightly flossing habit, and other habits spiral you in the wrong direction, such as smoking or eating fast food. You can increase the number of positive and healthy habits you have and decrease the ones that don't nourish you.

The experts say that it takes 21 days to form a habit;[3] that if you consciously practice something for 21 days, it will eventually become something you do unconsciously. For the purpose of making a point I'll be kind and give you 90 days. If you take just one suggestion from this book and apply it consistently to your life for 90 days, it will become a habit. Remember: habits require no conscious energy. Once you have your first habit down, you may move on.

On the ninety-first day you add one new habit, not two habits, and practice that for 90 days. At the end of six months you will have two positive new habits. If all you did was add a new habit every 90 days, in five years you would have accumulated 20 new, positive, life-inspiring habits that you wouldn't have had if you walked away and did nothing. How fabulous would it be to have your life running on autopilot in the direction of your goals and dreams?

This is not about deprivation, but growth. It is not about taking habits away, but about adding habits that strengthen your core. If you've always wanted to quit smoking, that may be too big of a challenge to start with. Instead start by adding apples to your diet. You know the saying, "An apple a day keeps the doctor away." There is something to that, and apples are very nutritious for you. Promise yourself to eat apples every day. Simple. Once that becomes a habit, work on adding a daily walk around the block. After 90 days of walking, you may find that you'd like to take up running. Before you know it, you will have accumulated so many healthy habits that smoking will seem ludicrous to you, and you will find the strength to quit. The more positive habits you add to your life, the more you will find the unhealthy habits miraculously fall away. It is about taking small steps every day that support your goals, so that one day you wake up and find you have been transformed.

Mark Twain once said, "Habit is habit and not to be flung out the window by any man, but to be coaxed down-stairs one step at a time."[4] It is my hope that through small consistent actions you will produce big results. It is a commonly held belief that if you consistently take good actions it will translate into good outcomes.

I am not a doctor, a nutritionist, or a physical fitness trainer. I am a regular person. Notice I didn't say "normal." I have a weakness for salty foods, I talk too much sometimes, and I have been known to have a bad temper. However, I have taken the advice I have accumulated over the years and I have learned that I can be healthier and happier, and mentally and spiritually fit by using the habits I am outlining in this book. I have been extremely fortunate in that I've spent most of my life educating myself for my work. I have read, studied, and applied the lessons from hundreds of books, articles, and seminars. I am a living test woman. I have pushed my body through physical exercise, challenged my mind to grow, and meditated on my faith. All of this has made me realize what works and what doesn't. What doesn't work are cosmetic fixes, fads, and miracle cures. What does work is steady perseverance and building yourself from the inside out. While not all of us have been given the same opportunities and privileges in life and experiences, we all have the same access to happiness. It is in our hands.

Our society would have you believe that it is the other way around.

The advertisers want you to think that if you buy their product your life will get better. If you only had longer eyelashes, a faster car, or a new nose, you would be happy. We are bombarded from the media with unattainable images of what beauty is. I know for myself that beauty and strength come from confidence. Confidence in knowing who I am at my core, and that I don't have to compete with the images I see. Happiness is not a competition. I am here to run my own race and so are you.

I have met so many women and men over the years in my seminars that don't have a strong core. From the outside looking in, they look good. They drive a nice car, have a nice appearance, work at a great company, but in their soul they are running on empty. They approach me on breaks or after class to ask for help, advice, and ideas. I have been asked over and over again if I had a book, and I didn't. Well I figured it was about time.

I once read a quote that said something to the gist of "one should never sit down to write until they have stood up and lived." I feel that I am in place now. Life has given me its share of ups and downs, and what has gotten me through and kept me strong are the habits I am going to share with you. These habits are everything from the habit of drinking water and habits about how you think to habits about how you deal with the challenges life presents to you. Having healthy habits results in a strong core.

When your core is strong, you have the confidence to pursue your passions, to connect with your purpose, and you have the power to perform whatever tasks are necessary to achieve your goals. When things do go wrong, you are able to hold things together and get back on track. Positive habits will liberate you and give you the strength to go forward no matter what.

So often I have witnessed people who have something bad happen in one area of their life and they let it overflow into every other area of their life. Dr. Martin Seligman explains in *Authentic Happiness* that even this has something to do with habits. Optimists and pessimists deal with the problems in their lives differently. They literally have different coping habits. He gives an example that goes something like this: Let's pretend that two people who work in the same department lose their jobs on the same day. The optimist is upset that she lost her job, but decides that she will make good use of her time off. She will get to the gym more often and try out some new meals on her family. The pessimist lets the loss of his job affect every other aspect of his life. He spends his time brooding and not participating in social events. He treats his family poorly, and thus the downward cycle begins and his bad habits spiral him down a negative path.[5]

The good news is that optimism can be learned.[6] The way you think is a habit, just like everything else. By incorporating one small change at a time you can totally transform yourself. I am going to introduce the many habits that make up my own life and then you choose. Some of the habits overlap and work together, and that is the beauty of them. You can adopt them by themselves, or build one on top of the other. This is about you, not me. I want you to feel more joy, passion, and purpose for yourself. Pick a new habit and try it on for 21–90 days. Don't do this stuff because I say so. Do it because you are ready for a change, and you be the judge. If it works for you, keep it and use it, and if you need to, modify it for yourself, or don't adopt it at all. At the end of the day I want you to feel better. Isn't that why you are reading this book? You want to experience life and you want to be fully alive, happy, and productive. You want your life to mean something. Well if you don't feel good, you won't do good. It is that simple.

The dictionary definition of the word "habit" is a settled or regular tendency or practice.[7] The cool thing about habits that is worth repeating is that they require NO energy. This is important to understand. Habits are the things you do without any thought or energy. As the old saying goes, "we create our habits and then our habits create us." If I was to come to your home and watch you get ready for work in the morning, over 50 percent of what you do is habit. You do the same thing every single morning. Yet you never sat down with a pen and a piece of paper and said to yourself, should I let the dog out first or brush my teeth? You just repeatedly did something and over time it became habit—something you do everyday that requires no thought or effort.

How have your current habits shaped you? Are your habits bringing you in the direction you want in life? If you changed nothing about the way you live your life, what would your life look like in five, ten, twenty years? What would the state of your health be? Your finances? Your relationships?

The even better thing about habits is that you create them. Keep the ones that serve you and rid yourself of the ones that don't by creating new and better habits. It also doesn't matter where you are in your life, the important part is which direction you are heading. You can be in a bad situation right now, but if you are heading in the right direction, going toward the light, and creating positive habits, you will soon come out on top.

We can all learn a lot from professional athletes. Think about how professional athletes prepare for their sport. They spend hours and hours practicing the fundamentals. They run the same drills and plays over and over and over again. A football team will repeat the same plays in practice until they are physically drained, winded, and spent. Each player is pushed to his or her physical and mental limit during practice. The players may want to stop, but the coach will make them run another play. Why do they do that? They do that so it becomes a habit. By practicing the same plays over and over, the team ingrain the plays so much in their brains that on game day—when they are on the field, on the court, and in the game—they are able to play effortlessly. Their brains have run this play, their bodies know they can do it, and their subconscious minds are able to take over.

The difference between athletes and the rest of us is that most of us don't spend the time and effort practicing our own habits—they just evolve without our conscious choice. Athletes spend 90 percent of their time preparing, practicing, and getting ready to be in the game. They only spend approximately 10 percent of their time on the court, on the field, and in the game. Most of us spend 100 percent of our time on execution, at work and at home, and we take little or no time to prepare and train.[8]

Okay, so you're not a professional athlete. Neither am I. The bottom line is that with a little consistent effort you can create positive habits. And the beauty is that once you create them, they are yours and they require no energy. Wouldn't it be great if you had so many positive habits that your life seemed effortless?

2

"Most folks are as happy as they make up their minds to be."

–Abraham Lincoln

Over the years people have often asked me how I stay so motivated and happy all the time. I am often asked how many cups of coffee I've had because my energy and enthusiasm is always at a peak. They usually scoff at me when I tell them that I don't even drink coffee (although I do now—a habit I recently developed in the last five years). Other times people will say, "I'd like to have some of what you're on." I used to tell people that I was high on life and leave it at that. I never thought about how or why I was happy. I just was. Looking back, I now realize that I was unconsciously happy.

In the past twenty years I have made tremendous changes in my life, and I began to become consciously aware of how I stayed motivated and happy. I have read countless books on what makes one person motivated and successful over another. I have been through some very tough years: job loss, divorce, stress, and soul-searching times. What I have found over and over is that truly happy people have a great deal in common. For starters, they like themselves and have created what I call "Happy Habits." Now even writing the words makes me cringe at the thought of how ridiculously corny that sounds, but I can swear to you that it is true. I also know I am the Queen of Corny, and I'm okay with that. The bottom line is your habits are linked to your levels of happiness, motivation, and success. I am not talking about faking it and masking all your problems; I am talking about truly being happy and grateful for all that life offers you. I am talking about paying attention to your habits and your perspective on your life, because this is your reality.

Life has also thrown me some tough circumstances in my personal and professional life in the past ten years. The tools or habits that I am writing about have been my saving grace and have been instrumental in helping me stay focused and motivated. I believe that these tools have given me deep roots and a strength I wouldn't have had had I not learned them in 1997 (see chapter 3). They have strengthened my core. My life is by no means perfect, but it is peaceful. The storms still come, the winds still blow, and things don't always happen the way I want. But since I have learned about the science of habits and applied it to my life, I am able to weather the storms and come out just fine on the other end.

After one of my first seminars, I was surprised when someone who looked as if they had everything going for them and everything together approached me to talk about something he was struggling with. This has happened so many times over the years that I can't count, and it has truly opened my eyes. Challenges come to us all, but the key is HOW you deal with them. I have come to the conclusion that no one escapes pain and bad experiences. Everyone has something they have to deal with in life. Pain just comes to each of us in different packages. Pain is not reserved only for the poor and destitute, and how we deal with pain will determine our level of satisfaction with life.

As a child, I unconsciously developed Happy Habits that were strengthening my core and I didn't even know it. Whenever I drew pictures I always drew hearts, flowers, and happy faces. I doodled the sentence "I Love Life" on every school notebook I ever owned. Some psychologist somewhere will probably tell me I was masking my sorrow, but it doesn't matter the reason. Little did I know that I was creating habits for myself that would last a lifetime. I unconsciously worked at surrounding myself with experiences that made me feel good as a child and young adult. I watched happy shows on television, I wore bright colors and listened to cheerful music. I covered my closet door with a collage of positive images that simply made me feel happy. At the time I did it because I wanted to and not because I had learned the power of vision boards or the effect of watching violence on TV or how listening to negative lyrics affects your mood. As an adult, I now know the power of these habits and apply them to my life regularly.

The naysayers of the world have told me that I must be so happy because I had a great childhood and that I didn't have any traumatic events happen to me. I didn't, but what does that mean? I know people who have had horrible things happen to them and they turned out fabulous, and on the other side of the coin, I know people who have had no trauma and they are a mess as adults. It really is more about how you deal with the events life hands you, versus what those events are. We have all had things happen to us in our lives that we wish we could have avoided. Our experiences shape us, but as adults we have a choice. We can continue to blame our parents for our lot in life, or our government, or our surroundings, or what school we did or didn't go to, or whatever else we can think of. Or we can take responsibility.

I was brought up in an average middle class family. I was brought up to believe I was a decent, average person and that I would make a decent, average living as an adult, just as my parents did. I came from a loving family that had its rough spots, but overall it was supportive. My parents believed in me and wanted the best for me.

I was a happy kid. As I carried this disposition with me into adulthood I was labeled a dreamer. I was told that I was not realistic and that I lived with my head in the clouds. I never let anyone's comments get me down. I liked being happy and enjoying my life. The bottom line was that I wasn't faking it. That was how I truly felt. It was genuine. As far as I was concerned, it beat being what I call a "dull normal." I define that as the mass percentage of the population that walks around complaining, blaming, and being unsatisfied with their lot in life.

I was once told after giving a training seminar that I was "too happy." Is there such a thing? I was just being me.

Once I had someone tell me to take my pom-poms and go someplace else when I said good morning to her. That was when I came to the realization that some people don't like happy people. We say we want everyone to be happy, but what we mean is that we want people to be happy when we are happy. We don't want any happy people getting in our face when we ourselves aren't happy. I learned that real quick.

I've watched people over the years who claim to be happy and positive, but if you followed them around for one day, you would find a totally different story. Why is that? Well to start with, we live in a negative society. The messages everywhere are negative. Television shows are negative, the news is almost 100 percent negative, reporters are always scaring us with another discovery that will compromise our health and infringe on our security, and even our friends, coworkers, and families are negative. Think back over the last 24 hours about the conversations you have had. Were they uplifting and positive or filled with dread and bad news? We are a society of complainers. We complain in the winter and we say it is too cold out. We talk about how long the winter is and how we can't wait for spring. Then on the first hot day, we complain that it is too hot. You figure it out.

I worked for a large corporation for many years, and I could swear to you that it was cool to be negative. When you came to work with something to complain about and wanted to vent about how bad your day was already going, you had a line of people willing to share a cup of coffee with you. But when you came to work happy, satisfied, and thrilled with your life, people weren't as eager to listen to you. I have had colleagues, when I started to talk to them, hold up their hands and say, "You're too happy and I haven't had my coffee yet."

In any event, I had made an unconscious decision early in life that has become a conscious decision later in life: to BE HAPPY. Happiness has less to do with what is going on in your external world and more to do with what is going on with you internally. Happiness is a state of being, not a place to arrive at.

3

"Don't ask what the world needs. Ask what makes you come alive, and go do it. Because what the world needs is people who have come alive."

–Howard Thurman[1]

The beginning of my conscious transformation began in 1997. The events of this year put me on the path to self-development and to consciously creating positive habits. I was always told growing up that I could be anything I wanted and that I was a great person. I believed that to a point. I believed that I could do anything within average standards. I never saw greatness for myself because I based my beliefs on the success my parents, grandparents, and aunts and uncles had created for themselves. That was my reality. I came from a working-class family. Work was something you did to make money. It wasn't a pursuit of your passion or purpose. Then my whole world changed in January 1997.

I had been working in the sales arena of a large company for almost ten years. I had risen steadily up the ladder to a position I was comfortable with. I never believed that I was going to be something more. Middle management was fine for me. I considered myself successful and was very happy with my life. I had a decent job, a fantastic husband, and a fulfilling family and personal life. What else did I need?

Then the company went through a downsizing and my position was eliminated. When I heard the news, I was devastated. I was a good worker, I did a good job, and, most important, I was extremely comfortable. I remember crying when my boss told me the news. I felt lost, cheated, and, well, average. I felt like I didn't matter. I was given 90 days to find another position within the company or I was out. Since I was in a vulnerable position, I settled for a job in the training department that I felt was beneath me. Previously I had been in a manager role and was paid a nice commission. This new job forced me to take a pay cut and give up my commission. It was a very humbling experience.

Yet after my first few months in my new job, I knew my life was about to take a different course. This position was a dream come true for me. For the first time in my corporate life I was truly comfortable being myself. In the classroom I allowed myself to be "myself." I actually found the more I let my true colors show, the more confident I grew, and the more value the participants got out of the classes I was leading. Like the quote at the beginning of this chapter, I had come alive.

This was one of the first aha moments in my transformation. I learned the habit of trusting the experiences life brought me, regardless of whether I liked them or not. I learned to trust that maybe the universe had a better plan for me than I had for myself. I realized in hindsight that having my job eliminated was the best thing that could have happened to me. Right now, I would like you to take a moment and think about the challenges you have faced in the past in your own life. Then I would like you think about the course your life took, after you made it through the storm. My hope is that, in hindsight, you too will see that your challenges have made you stronger and put you on a path you may have never taken on your own, and that given the chance to go back and change the events of your life, you wouldn't change a thing.

My second aha moment came when I went to Jack Canfield's seminar that summer in Santa Barbara, California, to learn about the secrets of success and how to develop healthy self-esteem. If my previous job had not been eliminated, I would have never taken a job in the training department. If I never took the job in the training department, I would have never known about Jack Canfield and been put on this path. When I attended his seminar, it was like a lightbulb exploded over my head and I got it. Jack taught me about the habits of healthy self-esteem.[2] He didn't call them habits, but I made the connection. Just like eating healthy and working out regularly keeps you physically fit, in order to be confident I had to work out my mind on a daily basis; I had to develop positive thinking habits. I found this wasn't too hard to do either. It didn't require that I count calories or that I get up an hour early to do sit-ups; it took a simple commitment to do something for myself everyday that fed my soul and lit me up. I only needed to develop the habit.

What I am going to present to you here is my core fitness routine and the habits that I have created for myself. I originally created these habits over fifteen years ago for personal reasons. I have been following them with the utmost dedication and it has truly affected my success. Being unconsciously happy was one thing, but being consciously happy is powerful beyond belief. Once you realize that your decisions and your habits are your choice and that you have the power to make and create them on a regular basis, your results will explode just like that lightbulb over my head.

4

Habit 1: Cultivate Patience

"When you lose touch with your inner stillness, you lose touch with yourself. When you lose touch with yourself, you lose yourself in the world."

—Eckhart Tolle[1]

When it comes to building habits, you need to trust the process and know that "These Things Take Time" (TTTT). Anything worth having takes time, and if your results are too quick, they most likely won't have a lasting effect. I learned this in my early twenties when I took up exercising. This was long before I attended Jack Canfield's seminar, and I hadn't yet made the connection between mental and physical habits, but that is the thing about life. When you reflect over all that you have experienced, you are able to connect the dots.

This story will illustrate my point about patience.

As a teenager and a young adult, I was not what I would deem fat, but I was a little overweight and very mushy, meaning I didn't have a great deal of muscle mass. At a time in my life when all my girlfriends could eat whatever they wanted and still look thin and beautiful, I was not so lucky.

During my freshman year of college I started starving myself in the hopes of achieving the thin body I craved. This is not a good habit to get into, and not something I would recommend, but there is a moral to my story. My diet consisted of cigarettes, popcorn, and FrozFruit (an ice pop with a lot of taste, but very little calories). My weight would go up and down five to seven pounds depending on the day, but I never experienced any real results.

A girlfriend suggested that I join a gym. I can vividly remember my first aerobics class. It was the eighties, and I clearly did not have a clue what I was doing. I wore the wrong clothes, and, since I was in such bad shape, I couldn't get through the class. I huffed and puffed and could barely keep up the pace. The skinny beautiful instructor made it seem so easy as she bounced and flitted around the room. Oh how I hated her but secretly wanted to BE her.

After class my face was bright red because I was so out of shape, and I couldn't breathe. I looked horrible. I turned the corner in the hallway of the gym and another girl looked at my red face and said quite frankly, "Oh good, you're out of the sunbed." I was never in the sunbed, but I looked like toast. Not a great first aerobics class experience.

I was, however, determined, and I kept coming back. I started reading Joe Weider's *Muscle and Fitness* magazine because my dad had them around the house. At the time there were no fitness magazines for women, and this magazine was aimed mostly at men, but it occasionally featured women. I didn't care. It inspired me. I cut out pictures of women's bodies that I admired (Corey Everson, Rachel McLish, and so on) and hung them on my closet door. I devoured articles and books on nutrition, and in the end I became the fit, pretty girl in the front of the aerobics class. As I said earlier, it isn't a competition, but it is about how you feel inside, and I felt great. Every body type is beautiful and has its own attractive attributes. Each of us needs to decide on our own definition of beauty for ourselves and then own our power.

Now this took a much longer time than I anticipated, and herein lies the lesson. I don't think I saw any real results in my body for the first year. I felt better, and I could feel that my cardio was getting better, but my body still looked mushy to me. I kept going and going and going, despite the fact that I didn't look any different. I knew somewhere deep down that I was getting better. I bought a quality gym for my home. I plastered my walls with picture of beautiful women's bodies. I wasn't going to ever be a body builder—or a model for that matter—and I knew that from the start, but the images motivated me. It was important for me to pay attention to how these photos made me feel. If they made me feel bad about myself, that wasn't my goal, and it wouldn't have worked. I told myself that I was exercising my heart and my brain. Since I wasn't seeing quick results in my body, I had to rationalize that I felt better, and my heart was getting stronger each day.

Then one day, over a year later, I noticed a hint of a muscle on my arm. Hallelujah! It was working. I have stayed consistent and, today, at 49 years old, I am very pleased with my strong body. I look good, I feel good, and working out is a habit for me. I don't think I have missed a week of working out in twenty years, barring a few injuries and illnesses along the way. It is part of my life. It is at the core of who I am, and over twenty years later it is something I make the time to do every week.

The moral of my story for you is to cultivate patience and perseverance to start slowly and build momentum. I want you to be successful and have some early wins right at the start. I want you to build your confidence and build your core one day at a time. If you attempt to change too much, too soon, you will fail early on. If you fail too early on in the process, you are more likely to give up. If you quit too soon, or expect instant results, you are only setting yourself up for failure. Be confident that if all you do is take one small step in the direction of your goal every day, you will be met with success.

The definition of the word "patience" means to tolerate delay.[2] I know that at your deepest level, you know if you take the necessary time, you will be met with success, and you will be able to set realistic expectations for yourself. Therefore, the first habit is the habit of patience.

MAKE it a habit

- Practice slowing down for a day and delaying gratification. Perhaps the next time you are at the supermarket, get in the longest line.
- Recall something from your past that was worth waiting for.
- Find a quote or a mantra you can say to yourself whenever you find yourself getting impatient and restless. Mine were "These Things Take Time" (TTTT) and "I can do this."

5

Habit 2: Get Enough Sleep

"Sleep is the best medicine."

—Dalai Lama[1]

Ay ay ay, I can already hear you moaning. Who has time to sleep? Most Americans are sleep deprived, overworked, and stressed out. I used to think sleep was a waste of time myself. I thought of all the things I could get accomplished if I didn't sleep so much. I tried to get by on fewer hours a night, but my body didn't agree with my plan. I even thought I could condition myself to need less sleep if I gradually got up earlier and earlier over time. That didn't work either. In the end I am a seven-to-eight-hours-a-night kind of girl. I can get by on five or six hours, but my head feels a little foggy and I don't perform at my best. I can feel the difference.

I suggest that you plan for sleep ahead of time. What do I mean? I mean think about what time you need to get up in the morning and count backwards. If you have to be up at 5:00 a.m., then you would commit to being in bed by 9:00 p.m. That is if you need eight hours of sleep like me. I suggest that you play around with how much sleep you actually need. You have probably gotten into a habit of having too little sleep, and you have learned to adapt. Listen to your body after a night of four hours of sleep. How do you feel? Do your muscles ache? Do you run for a cup of coffee? Do you feel lethargic? How do you feel after six hours of sleep? This is a personal decision, but make sure you are not kidding yourself. Believe me, I wish I could operate on less sleep. I am an excited person with tons of ideas and energy. If I didn't have to sleep so much, I could probably get more accomplished. Yes, I can function on a few hours of sleep a night, and no one would know any different, but I know I am not operating at my peak, and my body knows it too.

Unless you give your body the time it needs to recover, none of the other habits will do you any good. In order to make these habits work for you and to be a peak performer, you need vitality, energy, and a positive attitude, which you will not have if you need sleep. Sleep restores and refreshes you and gives you the energy you need to get through your day. A cup of coffee or a chocolate bar only has a short-term effect, and nothing replaces good old-fashioned sleep. Don't kid yourself.

When you are sleep deprived, your concentration and focus are impaired; you are grouchy and easily stressed. You become irritable, and you make more mistakes, cause accidents, and are overall not fun to be around.

When you do get enough sleep, you won't even need to use an alarm clock in the morning. I haven't used one in years. My body gets what it needs and then naturally wakes up within seven to eight hours after I've gone to bed. I awake feeling refreshed and ready to start my day.

I was fortunate enough to hear Dr. James B. Maas, the author of *Sleep for Success*, speak live, and he said that the hour when your body takes what you've learned during the day and moves that information from your short-term memory to your long-term memory and the hour when your body does most of its rebuilding is in your eighth hour of sleep. That information was amazing to me, especially knowing that most people don't get eight hours of sleep.[2]

Sleep will improve your memory, and if you aren't getting eight hours of sleep, you are not being all that you can be. But if you are really honest with yourself, you don't need an expert to tell you that you need sleep— you already know it.

When you get a good night's sleep, you wake up feeling energetic and you have a deeper sense of well-being. You are more focused, and as a result, you accomplish more in less time. So often I hear people telling me that they need more hours in their day, and I disagree. 24 hours is delivered to your door every day and it is a gift. Knowing what to do with it and having the energy to follow through is the secret. Sleep will do this for you.

One of my coaching clients swore to me that he didn't need over five hours of sleep a night. He boasted about how efficient he was and claimed that he felt fine on the sleep he was getting. Over the years he had gotten into the habit of going to bed very late. It was a rare occasion that he went to bed before midnight. When I asked him what he was doing in the evenings, he told me that when he got home from work he would unwind with the mail and/or the newspaper and a glass of wine. He would then eat a late dinner, and afterwards he would sit on the couch and watch television. I asked him if what he was watching was educating, motivating, or inspiring him, and when his answer was no, we decided that he would give up his nightly television habit and replace it with the habit of going to bed earlier. If there was something he really wanted to watch that was on later in the evening, he would record it and watch it the next day.

He committed to going to bed earlier and aiming for seven to eight hours a night for one month. At the end of the month he reported that he had more energy, and, surprisingly, without changing his diet, he had even lost weight. Two years later he is habitually going to bed earlier, and he claims that he has much more energy in the morning and he awakes feeling calmer and more focused. He started working out more consistently with his newfound energy and has dropped over twenty pounds in the last two years. I can't guarantee the same results for you, but I can guarantee that sleep will invigorate you and help you focus.

I have to add, after he lost the weight, I started to pay closer attention to my own eating and sleeping patterns, and on the nights I didn't get enough sleep, I found myself eating more than usual the next day. This was my personal observation, and it was a big aha moment for me. Tune into your own habits and you may be surprised.

All of which proves the fact that sleep will do you wonders.

MAKE it a habit

- Create a bedtime ritual one hour before bed that relaxes you.
- Turn off the computer, television, or anything electronic 30 minutes before bed.
- Go to sleep at the same time every night.
- Keep a journal by the bed and jot down any last-minute thoughts in an effort to free your mind for sleep.

6

Habit 3: Visualize Your Tomorrow Tonight

*"Visualize your dreams in living color and feel how you would
feel if your dreams were true before you drift to sleep at night."*

—Unknown wise person

Whatever your brain is focused on before you fall asleep is what your subconscious mind will process all night. If you spend the last few minutes of your day visualizing something positive and empowering, those are the thoughts your subconscious mind will process all night. The sad fact is the nightly news is the last thing many people end their day with. Think of all that bad news just spinning through your brain while you are asleep. No wonder so many people wake up still feeling depleted and exhausted.

Instead of watching the news, close your eyes and visualize what your intentions for the next day are, or the next week, month, or year. Visualization is the simple act of closing your eyes and imagining in full color what you desire for yourself in your mind. Your imagination is the one place you can do anything. You can jump, leap, dance, and even fly. Many people use their imagination to conjure up pictures of what they fear, but I am asking you to imagine what you want.[1]

Pick one or two areas in your life that you want to work on, and visualize what those areas would look like in a perfect world. If you would like more energy and enthusiasm for life, visualize that before you go to bed. For example, visualize yourself waking up in the morning with energy and enthusiasm for the day. See yourself opening your eyes with a smile, stretching, and getting out of bed with a purpose for your day. Imagine yourself walking to the bathroom mirror and smiling broadly at the image you see. Imagine getting ready for your day with a spring in your step, enjoying your morning cup of coffee, and leaving for work feeling calm and centered. Imagine walking into your office with a sense of anticipation and wonder over what the day has in store, and then imagine yourself calmly and intelligently dealing with every challenge that comes your way. What would that feel like? Close your eyes and focus on your senses. What would you look like if you awoke in the morning happy and energetic? How would your body feel? How would other people react to you? Visualize it all, from how you would greet yourself in the mirror to how you would greet your family and coworkers.

Olympic and professional athletes use visualization all the time. Michael Phelps, the Olympic swimmer who walked away with a record-breaking eight gold medals in a single Olympic year in 2008, said that every night before bed he visualized every stroke, every turn, and every flip. In effect he programmed his subconscious mind with what he wanted to achieve so when he got in the pool at the Olympic Games his body and mind operated on autopilot. He had swum those races in practice and in his mind millions of times before.[2]

Another way to use this habit is to visualize how you would feel after having the perfect day. See yourself walking to your car after a productive and satisfying day. Imagine you closed the deal, gave a fabulous presentation, or spent some quality time with your loved ones. Imagine how good you would feel after such a day. I had one of my clients who was preparing for a big presentation visualize how it would feel after giving a successful presentation. I had him visualize the drive home and focus on all his good feelings. He visualized opening all the windows in his car, feeling the breeze on his face, and singing at the top of his lungs. He imagined that once he got home, he and his wife sat down for dinner, opened a good bottle of wine, and toasted his success.

By doing this before you go to bed, you will set your subconscious mind to work. Just like an athlete that runs the same play over and over, you are visualizing your outcomes in your mind. I don't claim to know how this works, actually, and quite frankly, I don't care. I just know that it does work. It works fabulously. Your thoughts are energy, and with or without you even knowing it, your thoughts are creating your reality. Why not put the power of your thoughts to work for you while you are sleeping? You spend at least a third of your life sleeping, and this is the time your conscious mind shuts down and your subconscious takes over. It is like having your very own personal assistant who helps you create a fabulous day.

I am naturally a morning person. I get out of bed most mornings with a ton of energy and enthusiasm. By the end of the day, I am usually depleted from giving so much and my brain is tired. It is very easy for me to collapse in bed and just fall asleep, too tired to do anything else. How I changed this habit was to put a book on my pillow. The book is my all-time favorite, Og Mandino's *The Greatest Miracle in the World*, but you should choose your personal favorite. When I get into bed each night, I have to move the book over to get under the covers, and by doing this I am reminded to visualize my intentions for the next day. It doesn't have to be more complicated than that. I lie in bed and give thanks for all that I have and then visualize one of my goals in detail, as if it were already coming true. I use all my senses and work to feel the feeling I would have if my goals were already true, and then I drift off to sleep with a smile on my face and my goals on my brain.

Since I have adopted this habit, I practically leap out of bed in the morning. I always wake up to great ideas in my brain, and I have the enthusiasm to see them through. It is as if I have my very own set of angels that see what I visualize the night before, and then they plant ideas in my brain for me to act on the next day. I find myself waking up at my own pace, and as my mind becomes clearer, so do the ideas. Once I am fully awake and the ideas are clear, my excitement grows and I can't wait to start my day.

MAKE it a habit

- Keep a note on the nightstand that reads: "Create your tomorrow tonight."
- Using all your senses, visualize what you would like the next day to be like in vivid detail.
- Talk to your spouse about what you each visualize for yourselves the next day.
- Keep a book, a note, or some other reminder on your bed that you will have to pick up and remove before you get into bed. This will remind you to use the final minutes of your day wisely.

7

Habit 4: Inspire, Motivate, or Educate Yourself in the Morning

"Formal education will make you a living; self-education will make you a fortune."

—Jim Rohn[1]

Create an early morning ritual for yourself. Don't hit the snooze button four times and then grab a cup of coffee and rush to work. No, I wasn't following you this morning. That is what most people do. I suggest that you start your morning off slowly. Take some time to lay in bed. Give yourself five minutes to think about what your intentions are for the day. Say a prayer of gratitude, and make a decision that no matter what happens once you get out of bed, you will MAKE it a great day.

Once you are out of bed, or at least before you shower, take some time—an hour on a good day, but a half an hour is better than nothing—to read, journal, or meditate. I go back and forth between the three. The one thing I do focus on is making sure that in this hour I am doing something that inspires, motivates, or educates me. This is a habit I have committed to for over sixteen years. Depending on my schedule, I just make it work. During the years when I worked for a corporation, that meant getting up at five in the morning or earlier. When I was working full-time and going to school full-time for my master's degree, that meant waking up at four in the morning. I don't get to do it every day, and that's okay. I don't beat myself up. I do what I can. I don't keep track of how often I do it. I have just made it a ritual that I follow whenever I can. I so look forward to the days I can do it, and I really miss it on the days I can't. I travel a great deal for work, and some days it just isn't possible, and that's okay. It is like my morning nutrition, my hour of power. It is the best way to start my day. I find when I read something that inspires, motivates, or educates me first thing in the morning that I am off to a winning start. I feel more positive and hopeful for what the day may bring. If you think about how much time and attention you give to showering, doing your hair, and maintaining your appearance, surely you can see the worth in taking some time every morning to feed your mind, body, and spirit.

Words have power, and if you choose to fill your mind with positive uplifting words first thing in the morning, you will carry that emotion throughout your day. It is like setting your course for the day, and once you do this, the rest of your day will follow suit. Just like before bed, many people start their day with the morning news, the Internet, and social media sites. You don't need more bad news and updates from your friends—you need more inspiration, more encouragement, and more excitement to follow your dreams. That is what this morning habit will do for you. When you feed yourself a diet of positive words, spend some time in self-reflection, or meditate and clear your mind in the morning, you are building a strong core.

When I started this habit, I made a promise to myself that on the days that I read I would aim to read ten pages a day of something that inspired, motivated, or educated me. At the time, I hadn't read a nonfiction book in over ten years. Yes, you read that right. Ten years! Over the past sixteen years, I have read approximately 25 books every year, 98 percent of them nonfiction. The reason I share this with you is because I would have been the first person back then to tell you that it couldn't be done. I would have pulled out every excuse in the book why I didn't have time to read, journal, or meditate. I am telling you because I am living proof that it can be done.

Books will change your life. They will lift you up when you feel down, challenge your beliefs, and inspire you to go another mile. Just like food, you need a good diet of words every morning. You don't need to watch the news or listen to mindless radio. You need to be lifted up, nourished, and encouraged to face your day with energy and vigor.

Some days I read, others I sit with my journal and let my thoughts flow through my writing, and sometimes I just sit on my back deck looking out into the woods and meditate, visualize, and set my intentions for the day. The ideas I am sharing with you in this book are meant for you to customize for yourself. So try on different ideas for a few weeks and see what feels right for you. The idea is to start your morning on a good note.

Pay attention to how your day goes on a day when you completed your habit versus a day when you didn't. If it makes you feel more centered and strong, keep it up. If it just adds more stress to your life, let it go. I know when I read words in the morning that lift me up and I take the time to meditate, educate, and inspire myself, I feel more centered and alive. I can feel my blood start to pump and the excitement in my body rise. I can't wait to start my day and I feel great. It sets a great tone for the rest of my day.

MAKE it a habit

- Set your alarm for a half hour to an hour earlier twice a week for 21 days—note how your day goes when you do this.
- Start small with daily inspirational readings. (Keep the book on your nightstand.)
- Purchase a meditation tape or download one on your phone with 15–20 minute meditations on it to get you started.
- Select your clothes and have whatever you need for your day packed and ready to go the night before, which will free up some time for you in the morning.

8

Habit 5: Eat Breakfast

"The way you eat is inseparable from your core beliefs about being alive. Your relationship with food is an exact mirror of your feelings about love, fear, anger, meaning and transformation."

—Geneen Roth[1]

UGH! How many times have you heard that one? You know you should. Do you do it? That is the question. Coffee doesn't count as a meal, and as Michael Pollan says in his book *Food Rules*, "It's not food if it arrived through the window of your car."[2] What are you feeding yourself in the morning? If you are home right now, get up, go to your cabinet, and take out what you had for breakfast today. Did it come from the earth? Did it come in a box? What is the shelf life of your meal? If it came in a box, look at the ingredients. Are there over 80 words listed that you can't pronounce? This is not a book on what and how to eat, but if you answered yes to the last question, go out and buy Michael Pollan's *Food Rules* and start there.

If you want to have the strength to create positive habits in your life, you need energy and a focused mind. Eating breakfast is just as important as getting a good night's sleep. Pay attention to how you feel after a healthy breakfast consisting of natural foods from the earth, to the days you don't eat anything at all, to the days you eat a heavy meal loaded with preservatives and fillers. Do you notice a difference in your energy level? You be the judge. After you eat something, pay attention to what your body tells you. We all have different body types and requirements, but your stomach will let you know if it agrees with what you feed it. You just have to pay attention and listen.

Your body needs you to eat something within your first hour of waking up. The word "breakfast" literally translates to when you "break" the "fast" that your body has been on all night . . . breakfast. So many people skip breakfast, claiming that they don't have enough time, or my all-time favorite is the people who tell me they are trying to lose weight. When it comes to time, you have to make the time—it is as simple as that. As for weight loss, all the studies have proven that eating a healthy breakfast will keep you from overeating later in the day and boost your metabolism.[3] Eating a healthy breakfast starts you off on the right foot in the morning and is linked to having a better mood. In my heart of hearts, I believe you know this. The question then remains, why don't you do the right thing? Making the time for breakfast takes practice. Like anything else, it is a habit you can form.

Let's talk about some easy and healthy options. In the summer, fill your body with fresh berries and local fruits. Buy them and keep them on hand at all times. Fill a bowl with berries and keep them in the front of your refrigerator. If they are in arm's reach, you will eat them. Blueberries, strawberries, blackberries, and raspberries are all loaded with the anti-oxidants that protect your body from illness. You can eat them alone, or combine them with granola, yogurt, or soy milk. Make sure your cabinet is stocked with healthy cereals. How hard is it to pour a bowl of cereal in the morning? A freshly prepared egg with some fresh basil and tomato will make your tummy very happy in the morning. In the winter, go for hot cereals, oats and rice, and whole grains. Buy organic when you can and read the labels for sugar content and other things. A word of caution when buying breakfast foods or anything for that matter: if the company is making huge health claims, you probably want to be careful. No one has to tell me apples are good for me. I don't believe what I read on the front of the box until I read the ingredients on the side. You don't have to be hugely educated in reading labels. If you don't recognize and can't pronounce most if not all of the ingredients, beware.

The best advice I can give you on making this a habit for yourself is to stock up on healthy items. Keep them in your kitchen cabinet, at your desk at work, and even in your car. If you have healthy options available, you will be less likely to go to the drive-through or to the vending machine.

MAKE it a habit

- Buy healthy cereal, granola, fruit, and easy-to-prepare breakfast foods.
- Eat within a half hour of waking up.
- Keep healthy bars and nuts in your car for the times you leave the house on an empty stomach.

9

Habit 6: Juice When You Can

"Anything in life is possible if you make it happen."

—Jack LaLanne[1]

Juice. Yes, juice. You've heard it before: it's good for you. Jack LaLanne swore by it. In 1984, at age 70, "[While] handcuffed, shackled and fighting strong winds and currents, [he] towed 70 boats with 70 people from the Queen's Way Bridge in the Long Beach Harbor to the Queen Mary, 1½ miles."[2] Jack LaLanne lived a healthy life for 97 years, and that should be an inspiration to us all.

You might already own an expensive juicer. The question is, when is the last time you used it? I have a juicer, but I don't always use it when time is of the essence. What works for me when I am short on time is the blender. It's plain, simple, and easy to clean up. I don't care what you use, but I will challenge you to try to add juicing to your habits. Juicing allows you to consume an optimal amount of fruits and vegetables in an efficient manner. We have all heard the recommendation to eat six to eight servings of fruits and vegetables, but on most days, this can be difficult. Juicing gives you more of what your body craves, and it doesn't take as long as you think if you follow my recipe.

Here is my favorite recipe for the drink I've entitled Green Inspiration:

3–4 big leaves of kale (minus the stems)
A large handful of baby spinach
1 apple
1 banana
Approximately 1½ cups water
Ice as desired
Blend

Experiment, have fun, and try some new flavors. Most people eat the same vegetables all the time. Try some new things in your juicer or blender and you will add a wider variety to your diet. In one serving you are eating so many good, healthy nutrients that your body will be singing for you.

If you don't have a juicer, you can always get juice on the go. Many organic stores have a juicer and would be happy to make one for you. My only word of caution is to pay attention to what they put in it. There are many juicing places that display beautiful fruits and vegetables on their front counter, but those beautiful fruits and vegetables never make it to your drink. Instead they fill your glass with sugar substitutes, water, syrup, and I'm not even sure what else. What I do know is that this isn't what I'm talking about. The juice you buy should be made directly from the fruits and vegetables themselves and never need any sugary and syrupy additives.

How many times a week do you think you could dedicate to making yourself a juice? If you can only commit to once a week, that is better than no times a week. If you have to write it on your calendar until it becomes a habit, then do so. A friend of mine is a lawyer and has twin children, so you can imagine how busy she is. She cuts the fruit and veggies the night before and puts them in the blender and then puts the entire thing in the refrigerator. In the morning she simply adds water and blends. Each child gets a sippy cup full of Green Inspiration and they love it. If she can make time, so can you.

MAKE it a habit

- Invest in a good juicer or blender. Ask your friends what they would recommend.
- Put all your ingredients in the blender the night before and keep in the fridge.
- If you don't have time to do the juicing, commit to going to your local health food store to buy juice that they blend on-site. It may cost a bit more, but you are worth it.

10

Habit 7: Eliminate What Is Not Working

"How you spend your time defines what you value."

—Unknown wise person

If you have read this far and are still with me, congratulations! Now before I go any further, I am going to back up a little. So far I have told you to go to bed earlier; visualize before sleep and make time in the morning for self-education, breakfast, and juice. Before I tell you to add another thing, I am going to ask you to eliminate some things.

Take some time to review a day in your life. What are some of the habits that you don't need? For example,

- Watching too much TV
- Surfing the Internet and social media sites
- Staying out late, or just staying up too late doing nothing of value
- Drinking/eating too much in the evening
- Reading news that doesn't add to the quality of your life
- Being a slave to your technology, rather than being its master
- Running around all day in reactive mode, with no schedule or plan for yourself
- Trying too hard to be perfect, look perfect, and keep a perfect home

It's not that people have a lack of time, but a lack of priorities. What is important in your life? Take a moment to answer that question for yourself. Is it your family, your health, your career, your finances, something else, or all of the above? The next question I ask is, what are you doing to build your relationships, increase your health, advance your career, or plan for your future?

The typical response I get is: "I'm going to get to it someday." Translation: "Ah, ah, well someday I was going to get around to that, but right now I'm busy chasing my tail, running around all day with no plan, and just being reactive to the tornado of events and tasks that come my way."

Being busy does NOT equal being productive. Pay attention for the next week to the tasks, appointments, and events that fill up your day. Ask yourself the following questions:

1. How do I feel about this task, event, etc.?
2. Does this give me pleasure or pain?
3. Am I being driven by myself or by outside sources?

You may have just organized a fabulous fund-raiser for your favorite charity. Everyone had a great time, you raised a large amount of money, and overall it was a huge success. The question is, did you enjoying planning it? Was it fun for you or stressful? Just because something is meaningful doesn't mean it gives you joy. You have to be very selective of what you spend your time on. Time is the one thing that keeps moving forward and that you don't ever get back.

If you want to increase the quality of your life, you have to be willing to get rid of what isn't working. Don't follow the masses or, as my good friend calls them, the "sheeple" of the world. Most of what everyone is doing is wrong, not good for you, and not healthy. If you want to have a life of quality, you have to be willing to take a different route. The route of self-mastery is not always easy, but that is what makes it so fulfilling and worthwhile. Are you ready to give it a try? Practice saying "no" for the next 48 hours when someone asks you to do something. Timothy Ferriss calls this revisiting the terrible two's in his book, *The 4-Hour Workweek*, and he advises you to say "no" to everything that doesn't get you fired.[1] I suggest you take a good hard look at what you are saying "yes" to and say "no" to as much as you can. Don't feel guilty and don't feel you need to explain yourself. Taking care of yourself is much more important than spreading yourself so thin that you end up exhausted and sick.

Pay attention to what gets your attention, and decide for yourself if this is something you want to keep doing or stop doing. When you are watching television, ask yourself how what you are watching makes you feel. Does it educate, motivate, or inspire you? Does it drain or exhaust you? When you wake up in the morning, are you full of energy and enthusiasm for your day? Did you get a good night's sleep, or did you stay up late watching reruns? Does your home have to be perfect? Do you have to look perfect all the time? Do you spend all day giving to other people, and never take any time for yourself? Be honest with yourself and look for things to eliminate from your life that don't serve you or improve your circumstances. By ridding yourself of time wasters and things that aren't that important, you can make time for what is important. You don't have time to do everything, but you do have time to do what is important.

MAKE it a habit

- Watch your daily activities like a hawk and tune in to how they make you feel and if they add to your life.
- Answer the questions I've outlined in this chapter.
- Select 1–2 items that you are going to stop doing.

11

Habit 8: Move Your Body Every Day

"Those who think they have no time for bodily exercise will sooner or later have to find time for illness."

—Edward Stanley[1]

I recently completed a 140-mile bike ride from the west coast of England to the east coast in three days on a mountain bike, 150 miles if you count the times we got lost. Now, I have been working out for years, but I hadn't done anything this challenging in at least ten years. I have worked out consistently over the past 20 years, doing my hour or two workouts four to five times a week, but this was different and called for more stamina and endurance. In addition, I hadn't cycled a great distance in years either. I knew my body was fit, but I would have to do some additional training. The ride was scheduled for October 7, so in August I took out my bike.

I can tell you that I wasn't motivated to get on my bike. I love to rollerblade in the summer. I rollerblade at least twelve to fifteen miles almost every day in the warm New York months. I love the feeling of putting my blades on my feet, strapping my iPod to my arm, having the headphones in my ears, and flowing to the music around the lake. To me there is nothing like a 6:00 a.m. start, the sun rising over the lake, a new playlist streaming into my ears, and the moment that the music and my rollerblades become one and take on a life of their own. I literally feel a shiver of pure joy move through every inch of my body, and I look up at the heavens and thank God I'm alive. That is my passion.

While I was an avid biker years ago, ever since I discovered rollerblades, biking has become something I do for fun with other people, but blading is my true passion. So you can imagine my hesitancy to get on my bike on a warm sunny summer morning, when blading was calling me. I even tried to do both for a while, but I found that I was pushing myself too much, and only three weeks before the big bike ride I had a really hard fall while rollerblading. I was flying down a hill when I felt a leaf stick in my wheel. It stopped my wheels on a dime, and I knew I was going down. Both my feet came flying out directly in front of me, I put my arms back behind me to brace my fall, and I fell flat on my butt. *WHAM!* Ouch! Being an avid rollerblader, falling comes with the territory, and I was shocked at how well I fared on this fall. I hit the ground hard and escaped with only a few scrapes. I have experienced much worse injuries in the past. What I didn't realize was how hard I had bruised my tailbone. It would be over a month before I could sit normally again.

I was terrified to get back on my bicycle, fearing that my butt would be too injured to ride. Imagine my surprise when it wasn't. When you sit in a bicycle seat, you don't sit on your tailbone. So off on my bike I went in an attempt to train for my 140-mile journey across England. The first couple of days I rode a pretty flat trail by my house that would take me about 50 minutes. I did this for a week or two, and then Gary showed up to start training with me. He had done the Coast to Coast three times before and knew what I was in for, so he insisted training on hills. I didn't like this, and I found them quite hard at first. We would climb up what I thought was a huge hill, and when we would arrive at the top, he would tell me we were going to go back down and we were going to do it again. I thought he was crazy, but I did it. We then took a 60-mile bike ride in one day and I could feel my confidence growing. I continued to train and felt strong and ready the first day of the ride.

We were a group of thirteen—ten men and three women. We met in Whitehaven and dipped our bicycle tires in the Irish Sea, which is tradition, and then off we went. The first day was a glorious 60 degrees, bright and sunny, with breathtaking views. There were a couple of long climbs, but I managed them well and my body felt good. I was told that the first day was the hardest, so when I did it without any problem, I felt victorious. Little did I know what the next day would hold in store for me.

On day two, we awoke to rainy, windy skies and temperatures in the 50s. As bundled up as I was, I just couldn't stay warm. Everything I had on was drenched. My socks slushed about in my shoes, and my fingers grew numb from the cold. At times the wind was blowing the rain right in my face and I could barely keep my eyes open. I was miserable to say the least, and oh, did I mention the hills? The hills on day two were the longest and hardest I have had to climb in years. I rode the White Rim in Utah about ten years ago, and this compared to that in my memory. In total we climbed 4,782 feet on this day. The hills I had trained on were meek and small compared to these monsters. Gary knew what he was doing when he pressed me to train on hills.

Through my training with Gary, I knew that getting off my bike wasn't an option, so no matter how slow I rolled, I just kept pedaling. I would arrive at the top of a steep long hill, only to be greeted with another and yet another steep long hill. When we arrived at the top of one such slog in the rain and stopped at a café for a tea, my body was shivering with cold, and I was in a foul mood. "You can do this," I kept trying to tell myself, but my attitude was growing grim, as my body was chilled, cold, and tired. In hindsight I realized that I should have trained my mind as hard as I trained my body. My attitude ended up in the gutter that day, but in the long run, my body did me proud. It was hard and challenging, and at the end of the day I was tired, but never was any part of my body sore. I took that as a sign that I had trained well and prepared my body for this challenge.

The feeling of accomplishment I have will live on for a while, and I am excited to seek out a new challenge. Next time I will select a warmer, sunnier climate.

Working out is a gift you give yourself. It is the gift of movement, the gift of life, the gift of being able to complete your daily activities without pain, play with your children, and dance with your lover. Just do it! Nike knows what they are talking about.

What better investment can you make than in the most important person in the world—yourself, your own body, and your well-being? You are no good to anyone in your life if you don't take care of yourself. Movement is life. Once you lose your mobility and stop moving, it is all over for you. It is simple: the more you move your body, the better it performs for you and the better you feel.

Years ago I read an interview with Gabrielle Reece (professional volleyball player), and she said her goal was to do something that moves her body everyday,[2] and I adopted that philosophy. If you think you are going to find the time, give it up. You won't. You have to MAKE the time, just like you have to MAKE it a great day!

The goal is simple: try and move your body for at least an hour as many times a week as you can. Your body is a miracle and built better than any machine ever made. After running a machine for a certain amount of time, the parts will rust, wear out, and break but when you work on a muscle, it only gets stronger, better, and faster.

I often read the Q&A columns in health magazines and people ask questions like, "should I work abs before shoulders," "do I do cardio before weights," blah, blah, blah. Stop complicating matters and just do something! The rest will come when you gain energy, strength, and knowledge.

Aim for at least four to five times a week. I find this to be easily accomplished. Look at what your week looks like ahead of time and plan your workouts before the week begins. If you can't make a workout or have a busy week, don't beat yourself up. Life sometimes gets in the way, and that is okay. You don't need to buy any fancy gadgets or magic products that claim to whittle your waist in 30 days. There are so many products claiming this or that, and I have found that you don't need any of them. Nothing beats good old movement done on a consistent basis. That means every week of your life, not just before bathing suit season or your high school reunion. Make a commitment to yourself that you don't want to have a "fat" wardrobe and a "skinny" wardrobe. A lot of you know what I mean. Decide that you want every season to be swimsuit season. You want to be able to put on your swimsuit in the middle of winter and be happy with how it fits. This is a lifestyle commitment.

Take a minute and think about exercise activities you love and that are fun for you. If you can't think of anything, that's sad. There is so much to choose from. It is as simple as putting on your sneakers and taking a walk on a beautiful morning. Do you love music? Any activity that feels like dancing is fun and doesn't feel like exercise. You can enjoy zumba classes, aerobics classes, rollerblading—even boxing has a cool rhythm to it. Over the years I've tried windsurfing, scuba diving, snow skiing, water skiing, mountain biking, street biking, ice-skating, boxing, hiking, paddle ball, salsa dancing, yoga, kettle bells, and a variety of other sports. Some I loved more than others, and those are the ones I practice today. You don't know what you like unless you try, and your age is irrelevant if you have passion for what you are doing. I have skied down the toughest slopes with people in their seventies, and they were skiing better and with more skill than me.

Take out your calendar and schedule your workouts just like you would an important meeting or a dentist appointment. Don't exercise just for the sake of exercising. It will be boring, tedious, and you won't stick to it. Be creative, get outside, try a new sport, work out with a friend, or join a running or hiking club. If you can find a friend to share an activity with, that is even better. If you don't have a friend that has the same interests, make new friends. With the Internet and meet-up groups, there are no excuses. My sister, who hadn't been exercising in a while, downloaded an app that helped her get fit for her first race. Each day the app walked her through a series of exercises with the goal of getting her from the couch to her first 5K. She loved using it and was a bit sad when she completed the last exercise. The best part was that it motivated her to start and kept her on track. I suggest you pay attention to what works for you. I find that there are times that I like to be with others and times that I like to be by myself with nature, God, or my music. With exercise, the cool thing is that you get an immediate benefit and a feeling of accomplishment. When you exercise your body releases endorphins. This is the chemical in your body that makes you feel good. Exercise is literally a natural high. Better yet, the lasting effects of exercise work to your advantage over time.

Our body is our power, and it has the ability to get you through anything if you feed and nurture it. It always amazes me how good I feel after a workout or after spending some time in the fresh air.

Taking care of your body with exercise will make you feel outstanding and it will give you the same benefits as a prescription antidepressant. A study published in the Archives of Internal Medicine in 1999 found that "Aerobic exercise was just as effective at treating depression as was Zoloft, or as a combination of exercise and Zoloft. Yet exercise is a lot less expensive, usually with no side effects apart from soreness."[3] Exercise builds your bones, reduces stress, and helps control your weight (but you already knew that).

In addition, people who exercise are happier. It feels good to experience getting better at something and to notice improvements in your performance and in your body. The longer you do something, the better you get at it, which leads you to not only feeling better but to being more confident as well.

MAKE it a habit

- Start small—work out once or twice a week.
- Make an appointment with yourself on your calendar.
- Find a workout buddy.
- Log your workouts so you can see your results.
- Get an app for your phone that tracks your progress.

12

Habit 9: Listen to Audiobooks in the Shower

"All wish to possess knowledge, but few, comparatively speaking, are willing to pay the price."

—Juvenal[1]

O kay, so it doesn't have to be in the shower, but make sure you listen. The reason I suggest the shower is that most people spend some time in the bathroom everyday getting showered and ready. You can turn your bathroom into a university. You can use the same theory in your car, or while walking, or riding the train. I find the shower works great for me. It allows me to multitask: showering while at the same time educating myself. If you are one of those people who uses the excuse that you don't have time to read, this is your solution. It requires no more time than it does for you to shower and get yourself ready in the morning.

The cool thing about listening is that you actually bring the voice and the energy of the expert right into the privacy of your own home. Just like a phone call connects you on a different level to a person than an email, an audiobook does the same. You will feel connected to the author on a higher level when you hear his or her voice. When you listen to something that educates, inspires, or motivates you, it engages your endorphins and you get excited to start your day. You will find that you experience a great surge of energy on the mornings you listen to audiobooks. If you dread long drives, and have a good audiobook, you will now actually look forward to them. When you have a good audiobook on hand, the drive seems effortless and enjoyable. This even works while stuck in traffic and makes the time much more tolerable.

The same rules apply with audiobooks as for real books, in that it has to be a topic that interests you. I don't believe anyone should suffer through something that isn't giving them enjoyment. However with the endless list of authors and choices, I do believe that everyone can find something they enjoy. You can subscribe to audible.com and pay for a one-year subscription in advance. By paying in advance, it will motivate you to not let that money go to waste. Audible.com is a site similar to amazon.com, only all of their books are audiobooks. Sometimes, after I've read a really awesome book, I will then download the audio version and listen to it a few times while out on my hikes or driving. I can see a noticeable difference in how I feel when I am in the middle of listening to a great book. It lifts me up and gives me energy.

I want you to note the difference in how you feel on a day when you've taken the time to listen to something that inspires, motivates, and educates you versus a day you opted to turn on the news in the morning. I think you will see a measurable difference in your overall energy and attitude.

MAKE it a habit

- Download an audiobook to your phone, iPod, or other device.
- Buy a subscription to audible.com.
- Keep a speaker for your iPod in your bathroom.
- Listen to audiobooks at different times to see what works for you.

13

Habit 10: Guide Your Thoughts All Day Long

*"As a single footstep will not make a path on the earth, so a
single thought will not make a pathway in the mind. To make
a deep physical path, we walk again and again. To make a
deep mental path, we must think over and over the kind of
thoughts we wish to dominate our lives."*

—Henry David Thoreau[1]

Your thoughts are the ultimate creator of your life. Consciously start
to pay attention to the voice in your head, if you haven't been already.
Unconsciously we are all listening, but power comes with conscious guidance. Think of all the thoughts you have all day long. Picture a radio dial
with lots of stations to choose from and a lot of chatter. You have control
over what station you listen to. Each station represents your thoughts, and
just like on your radio dial, you can only listen to one station at a time.
Your conscious mind can only hold one thought at a time, and if you
really think about it, you have control over what that thought is,[2] just like
you have control over what radio station you listen to. Our brains are the
most fascinating computers on the planet, and they only know what you
tell it. What have you been telling your brain all your life? How would
you even know? If you stop long enough and pay attention, you will hear
what station you have tuned in to.

Listen to your self-talk. Your self-talk is that voice in your head that is
constantly chattering at you. If you find yourself saying, "my who?" listen
up. When I am giving my live seminars, I always ask to see a show of
hands of who talks to themselves. Usually almost every hand in the room
goes up, with the exception of one or two. I then make the statement
that the few people who didn't raise their hands are saying to themselves,
"Talk to myself? I don't talk to myself." It always gets a roar of laughter.

You see, we all have this little voice in our head that is talking to us nonstop all the time. The question is, what is it saying? Is that little voice telling you how great you are and making you feel good about yourself? Or is it just the opposite?

What is it telling you? Studies have shown that 80 percent of the time that little voice is being negative.[3] It is saying things to you like, "I wouldn't do that if I were you." "People will laugh at you if you do that." "Stay over here where it is safe." If you don't take the time to discipline your mind, then it is always working to keep you safe. Unfortunately, at the same time it is keeping you from growing and becoming all that you are capable of.

Once you stop and listen to your self-talk, or your "inner critic" as it is sometimes called, you will realize the job ahead of you. Your thoughts and the words you speak to yourself set the direction of your life like the sail on a boat. Where are your thoughts taking you, and who is steering the ship? To change your life, you must first change your thoughts. Once you realize that your thoughts are like those radio stations and that you are in control, you have power. You decide whether or not you are going to listen to the station that beats you up and tells you what a loser you are, or if you are going to tune into the station that tells you that you are a winner and that you can accomplish whatever you put your mind to.

If your conscious mind can only hold one thought at a time and you have control over what that thought is, don't you want to make sure you're thinking thoughts that will help you?[4] The one thing you have as a human being is free will and choice. Every thought has an opposite thought. You can dwell on the fact you are overweight, or you can dwell on the fact that you desire to be thin. You have choice. Whatever you focus on grows, and a belief is only a thought that you keep thinking over and over. You can guide your thoughts toward what you want. Brilliant! You can direct your thoughts to support you in achieving your goals. The more attention you give to a thought, the stronger it becomes. It is actually impossible to stay in a bad mood if you keep flooding your mind with positive, empowering thoughts.

Know that at any time and at any place you can choose to let go of thoughts that don't serve you and choose thoughts that do. Remember the radio station. When a song comes on that you don't like, you change the station. Do the same thing with your thoughts, and once you do, your emotions will follow.

You are what you feel and think about.

If over the years you have had no experience in disciplining your mind, there is help on the way. Now you can't change everything overnight as I said earlier, but you can change your direction overnight. Pay attention to your self-talk and then apply the following guidelines if needed:

1. Acknowledge when your self-talk is holding you back. Be aware and conscious of all the limiting beliefs it instills in you.
2. Ask yourself how this belief is limiting you from having what you want.
3. Ask yourself what belief you would need to have to get what you want.
4. Replace the limiting belief with the more empowering belief.
5. Affirm and visualize your new belief (more about both in later chapters).
6. Repeat, believe, practice.
7. Take action.

A client of mine wanted to get a promotion, but the voice in her head wasn't serving her. She knew she was capable of doing the job, but the voice in her head kept belittling her. It would say, "Who do you think you are? You don't even have a college degree." Ouch. If she listened to that voice, she would have never gotten anywhere. Instead she chose to change the station.

Her goal was to grow her confidence and her belief in herself. So whenever she heard the voice in her head telling her that she wasn't good enough (Step 1), she decided to do something about it.

She used the steps above and practiced how she spoke to herself. She realized that if she continued to listen to the voice in her head that was telling her she wasn't qualified for the job, she would never get anywhere (Step 2).

She asked herself what she would need to believe about herself to move forward (Step 3).

She identified that she would have to believe she was qualified to fulfill the requirements of the job based on her experience and not on whether or not she had a degree.

She created a new affirmation for herself, stating, "I am more than qualified to succeed in my new role as Marketing Director" (Step 4).

She wrote down her affirmation, she repeated it to herself every morning, and she took action by letting the right people know that she was interested in the position (Steps 5, 6, and 7).

The negative part of your self-talk is your ego speaking, and you are NOT your ego. The ability to separate yourself from this voice in your head is what will free you. Once you realize that you ARE NOT the voice in your head and that you don't have to believe every thought that you have, then you have choices, which leads to peace of mind and freedom. At this point you can then use your brain for constructive and fabulous endeavors.

Every moment you have a choice about what you will think and what you focus on. In a matter of seconds you could go from laughing to crying based on what you are thinking, and vice versa. When you find yourself upset, frustrated, or stressed out, take a step back and pay attention to what your mind is focused on. If it isn't a thought that empowers you, realize that you have the power to choose another thought. That is what I mean by guiding your thoughts. This is not something you do for 90 days and then stop. This is something you do every day a million times a day for the rest of your life. The more you do it, the better you will get at it, but it is a lifetime commitment.

The better you get at this, the richer your experiences become and you realize that your limiting thoughts and beliefs were holding you captive. Your thoughts are the ultimate creators of your life, and you have control over them. Every thought you have vibrates and has an energy to it. Who you are is determined by what you think, like it or not. The longer you ponder a thought, the stronger it becomes. Studies have shown that even though the average person has sixty to eighty thousand thoughts a day, most of us are just rethinking the same thoughts day in and day out.[5]

Go back to the radio station example and realize that you may not be able to stop a self-defeating thought or song that you don't like coming on the station, but you decide if you want to stay on that station or choose another thought or song.

If you think you can, or you think you can't, you're right.

—Henry Ford

The more you focus on what you want, the more you will get what you want. So many times people say they don't want to be sad, or broke, or sick, but they don't realize that that is what they have been focusing on day in and day out. You are the living balance of what you have been thinking. Every thought has two sides, as I said before—the version that you want and the version that you don't want. For example, if you are trying to lose weight, you can choose thoughts of how you will feel in your new healthy body, or you can dwell on how fat and uncomfortable you feel now. You have a choice: two versions. Make sure that you are focused on the choice you want to manifest and not its opposite.

In Jill Bolte Taylor's book, *My Stroke of Insight*, Jill finds herself having a stroke at age 38. She is a Harvard neuroscientist, and because of her training she realizes that she is having a stroke, but she can't do anything about it. She ends up losing the left side of her brain for almost eight years. What does this have to do with anything, you ask? Everything, I say. Our left brain organizes the details of our lives. It tells us that there is a past, present, and future. It tells you to put on your underwear before your pants, and it recognizes patterns. It is where language exists, it tells how letters make words, and it is mathematical. In our right brain there is no such thing as time. There is only this moment, joy, imagination, and no inhibitions. There is no judgement or ego in our right brain—just love.

When Jill finally does recover her left brain function, she realizes that she has a choice. She doesn't have to recover some of her old thoughts and beliefs, especially the ones that didn't serve her. She then makes a conscious decision to not connect to her stubbornness, criticism, or grudges. For the first time she realizes that these are the choices she had made before, and she doesn't have to make them anymore.[6] What emotions do you not want to give life to anymore? Why not let go of jealousy? How about fear, loneliness, and arrogance? I can make a list for myself, but you have to answer this question for yourself. The next time you find yourself feeling any of the emotions that don't serve you, remember that you can choose another thought and your emotions will follow.

Your positive thoughts should outweigh your negative thoughts. If you spend only an hour a day praying, being positive, and meditating and then go out in the world and moan, groan, and complain all day, that is the world you create for yourself. You don't get what you want; you get what you dwell upon all day long. Whatever you focus on grows, and you give it power. You don't have to think thoughts that bring you down and bring you pain. You can choose peaceful, centered, and loving thoughts.

In Bruce Lipton's book, *The Biology of Belief*, he explains, much better than I ever could, that your genes are listening to everything you say, think, and do, and they are responding accordingly. This science is called epigenetics, and it says that our genes are merely the blueprints for our body and that every thought we have sends a signal to our genes. Our cells have been proven to move toward positive stimulation and away from negative. Therefore, every thought you have is sending a message to every single cell in your body. Choose thoughts that light you up and make you believe in yourself.[7]

Try this right now: If you want to be happy, choose a happy thought or a happy memory, or envision a happy future, and your whole body will begin to feel happiness and joy. The longer you ponder the thought, the better you will feel. The same is true if you want to feel sad, if you want to feel worthless or unimportant. Given the choice, I choose to consciously guide my thoughts toward things that empower me and make me feel worthy.

This is hard at first, I know, but over time optimistic thinking will become your habit and will require no energy. It will be natural to you. The only time you will have to call on your conscious mind is when you find yourself stressed or worried. You can step back and ask yourself the questions again.

MAKE it a habit

- Pay attention to your thoughts for 24 hours. Are they helping or hurting you?
- Imagine your brain is a radio station and make sure you tune in to an uplifting station.
- Choose a powerful and positive thought.
- Have a conversation with yourself and ask for support and guidance.

14

Habit 11: Have a Clear Vision and Goals

"If you are not working on your ideal day, you are working on somebody else's."

—Marjorie Blanchard[1]

When I graduated from college with my bachelor's degree, I had it in my head that I would like to get my master's degree. My boyfriend at the time, who later became my husband, had taken one flying lesson and told me that he wanted to get his pilot's license. This was in 1987, and for ten years all we did was talk about it . . . blah, blah, blah. It sounded great coming from our mouths, but we hadn't done a single thing to make it a reality. The thing with a goal is you have to back it up with a plan. I didn't have a plan for going back to school, and so year after year, my goal went unfulfilled. Then in 1996 I learned about goal setting. That is sort of the truth. I had known about it for a long time, but I didn't think I needed to set goals. My life was going along just fine. Up until then I had achieved everything I had wanted. I got my college degree, met and married a great man, bought a charming home with a great piece of property, and went on fabulous scuba diving vacations at least twice a year. Life was good and I was happy. Who needs goals?

In 1997, I was motivated to give goal setting a chance. The question was, what did I want? I really didn't know the answer to that question. Oh sure I could give the stock answers: "I just want to be happy. I just want to be healthy. I just want to be financially secure." But what did that really mean? What does happy look like and how do I know when I've arrived? I didn't have the answer to those questions, and no one had ever asked me before.

So I decided to start small. One of the first goals I set was to read more books. I also decided that I would start to research some master's programs. I had only been talking about it for ten years. I set a goal to be enrolled in a master's program by such and such a date. Notice, I didn't say graduate. I was so afraid of goal setting, and I didn't know what I was doing. I didn't want to set myself up for failure. I encouraged my husband to join me and to set a goal to get his pilot's license. I was excited about this goal setting methodology and my excitement was contagious.

I remember distinctly the Saturday morning Stephen took me flying after he got his pilot's license, because it was the morning that John F. Kennedy Jr. was killed while flying his wife and her sister to Kennebunkport. We went out to Teterboro airport in New Jersey and everyone was all abuzz saying that he was missing. No one really knew what had happened yet, just that his plane was lost. It was a swelteringly hot day with no relief. We climbed into the Cessna, which I called a Volkswagen with wings because it is so small, and we took off. We weren't going anywhere specific—just for a ride. We lived in Rockland County, not far from the airport, and Stephen wanted us to fly over our house. When we got in the vicinity, he said, "Look for the house." I did, but then I was confused. There was what looked to me like a huge tarp on the lawn and a bunch of people. It took me a minute to focus before I realized that the tarp was actually a sign that read "Congratulations, Michele," and all the people were my family and friends. You see, Stephen had gotten his pilot's license and I had gotten my master's degree! Only two years after giving the goal a deadline, it had become reality. After ten years of only talking about it. That is the importance of giving your goals a deadline.

Over the years people have said to me, "What if I fail? What if I don't make the deadline?" And I always answer back, "What if you do?"

What do you want for yourself? What is important to you? What do you value in life?

This is very personal and something no one else can answer but you. Don't worry about what your spouse thinks, what your mother wants for you, or what your boss thinks you should want. What do you want?

Think back to ten years ago. What did your life look like? What kind of car were you driving? Where did you live? Were you in school? Were you working? Married? Did you have children? In general, what was going on in your life? Take a minute to reflect and think about this. Don't skip this part. Put the book down, and get a clear image in your mind of your life ten years ago.

Did you take a moment? Good. Now ask yourself where you see

yourself ten years from today. Where will you be living? What will you be doing? Who will you be doing it with? Use your imagination and don't be afraid to say what you really want. Jot down some of your ideas in the space provided below.

_____

_____

_____

_____

_____

_____

What is going to help you achieve what you wrote down? If you answered goals, you're right. Goals will help you get what you want. Most people don't just show up at the New York City Marathon without preparing in advance. Life works the same way. In order to achieve what you want, you must first know what you want, define it, and write it down. It is that simple. You don't have to make it any more complicated than that. There are all sorts of different methods to goal setting, and they all work. I don't want you to get caught up in the technique if you've never set goals before. I just want you to keep it simple for starters.

1. Decide what you want
2. Write it down as specifically as possible
3. Give it a deadline for completion

Figure out what you want and write it down. Be as specific as you can, because that helps your brain help you get what you are looking for. The reason for being specific stems from the fact that there are so many things fighting for your attention out in the world, and our brain can't take them all in at once. Because of this we form scotomas on our brain. That is just a fancy word for blind spots. You've heard the saying, "You get what you are looking for"? Our brain is fascinating and it aligns what we see with what we know and what we are looking for. Just think back to the last time you purchased a new car. What did you see the next day on the road? Cars like yours. They were everywhere. Did they have a sale on your car? NO. You just had a blind spot and your brain wasn't registering those cars in your brain until you got one. The same thing happens with goals.[2]

When you write down that you want a new car, that could mean any car, but if you write that you want a black Mercedes convertible, your brain will start to focus you on Mercedes advertisements, deals, and showrooms. The same is true if you set a goal to be healthy. What does healthy mean? How will you know when you achieved it? What does healthy look like to you? This is where getting specific will help you in attaining your goal. If you set a goal to eat three vegetables a day or complete one hour of cardio three times a week, you now you have a specific health goal you can work toward.

Once you write them down and get specific, your brain starts to help you see what you are looking for.

You did get the part where I said write it down, yes? That is a huge part of goal setting. We all spend a lot of time hoping, wishing, and praying for things that we make no effort to move toward. For this reason, our brain doesn't always take us seriously. It has heard you say things like "I wish I was rich" or "I wish I weighed less" over and over, and yet you haven't done anything to work toward that goal ever, so your brain doesn't take you seriously. There is something about when you put a pen to paper that your brain believes much more than a simple wish. When you commit a goal to paper, your brain stops and thinks, "Wow, they're serious. Let me see what I can come up with to help them."

After you have written it down, set a deadline for completion. This is the most important part of goal setting. Without a deadline, it will always remain a someday item on your life list and you may never achieve it. When you write down a date, you will start to feel butterflies in your stomach because you know you now have work to do. You can't just sit around wishing anymore—the date motivates you to take action.

That's all you need to know to get you started with goal setting. Many people have told me that they don't set goals because they are afraid of failure. There is no such thing as failure. If you don't own a Mercedes convertible now and you set a goal and you never own a Mercedes convertible, you didn't fail at anything. You are still in the exact same place as when you started. If you don't hit the mark on your first try, then try again and again and again.

I am going to add some additional suggestions here, but start where you are comfortable. I believe that a good goal should give you butterflies and make you a little uneasy. It should stretch you out of your comfort zone a little. If your goal is making you sick to your stomach, maybe you bit off more than you can chew, or maybe you just need to break it down into smaller steps. For example, if one of your goals is to run the New York City Marathon and you are overweight and have never run before, a series of smaller goals should be set building up to the big goal. Start with walking or running a mile two times a week, and then build up your endurance from there.

If your goal is still making you sick to your stomach, you have to get real honest with yourself. Do you really believe this is possible for you? If the answer is yes, break it down into steps as I suggested. If you are six feet two inches and you always wanted to be a ballerina, that may not be in the cards for you. If your goal is really out there, and you believe it, I say go for it. The Wright brothers believed they could fly, Kennedy believed the space program could put a man on the moon, and Roger Bannister believed he could break the four-minute mile record for running, even though every doctor and expert said it was impossible. Even though all of those things had never been done before, the people who made them happen didn't let doubt enter their mind. If your goals aren't that lofty, that's fine too—the key is to have goals to work toward.

Be sure that the goals you chose are the ones you want to accomplish. Many people strive for goals that aren't even theirs. This is what I refer to as the unspoken rules of society or Picket Fence Syndrome. Many people strive to get married, have children, buy a house and a fancy car, and achieve money, beauty, and fame, but they never stop and ask themselves if that is what they want. So I am here to ask you: What do you want? What will make you happy?

It is a good idea to vary the types of goals you set. Based on the types of goals you set, you will achieve varying levels of happiness and satisfaction.

Here are some sample goal categories:

Health and Fitness	Family and Relationship
Material	Financial
Career	Spiritual
Personal Development	Fun and Leisure
Experiential	Learning

Review your goals and ask yourself, are your goals materialistic, like a new house or car, or are they experiential, maybe a trip somewhere? Do they make you a better person or teach you a new skill? Do they help you grow? Are they connected to your purpose? There is nothing wrong with any of these categories, but you would need a mix of goals to derive long-term satisfaction.

Buying a bigger house will make you happy for a little while, but eventually it will lose its effect. The quest for material objects, money, and power doesn't fulfill us in the end because we always want more. Learning a new language can be very satisfying, but it depends how you approach it. You can get an A on the Spanish test but still not know how to speak the language.[3] I spent four years studying Spanish as a student. I passed all my exams, but I still walked away not knowing how to speak Spanish. Is your goal to get an A on the test, speak fluently, or both?

Studies have shown that goals that help us grow and are activity based, such as taking up a new sport or hobby, give us more satisfaction over time and make us happier.[4] That is not to say that you shouldn't strive for the house and the car—just that you shouldn't make that your ultimate and only goal. We have all seen people, especially in the media, who from the outside look like they have it all. They have all the outward signs of success: the car, house, and career. What we don't realize is they still may not be happy with who they are on the inside. That is why I strongly encourage you to have a variety of goals.

Some goals are ongoing and never really get completed. A goal to live a healthy lifestyle is one you must practice your entire life. It is not a goal to arrive at or something to complete. A goal to practice yoga is a proficiency goal and also unending. You can practice yoga for years, and it may give you a lot of satisfaction in the long run, but it will never be completed. You are always learning and growing in proficiency. When you are focused on a proficiency goal, you don't have to prove you are perfect. You are going through a process, and with a process your perspective changes. You allow yourself to make more mistakes, you give yourself time to improve, and you don't give up. Proficiency can be painful and take time, but in the long run it will give meaning to your life and make you feel good about how far you have come and what you have accomplished.[5]

I believe we all have goals and dreams in our heads. Some that we fervently go after and some that we are afraid are a bit too lofty to ever come true. I believe that the dreams in your head are there by no accident. I believe if a dream has been taking up space in your head, you are the one that is supposed to make it come true. The question is, how long are you going to wait? Take the time now and turn that dream into a goal.

Once you take the time to turn your dreams into goals, you'll have a blueprint for your life. Having goals will provide you with a direction and a sense of purpose. In Dan Buettner's book *The Blue Zones—Lessons for*

Living Longer from the People Who Lived the Longest, he states that one of the things that kept people healthy and living into their hundreds was a sense of purpose coupled with a positive attitude. It gives you something to work toward and a reason to get up everyday. This in turn raises your confidence and your belief in yourself.[6]

Goals that support something bigger than yourself have been proven to add meaning to your life, and meaningful goals fill you up on a much bigger level than materialistic goals. For example, if your talent is teaching and you make it your goal to use this skill to help children learn to read in low-income communities, you will achieve greater fulfillment in the achievement of that goal and your personal satisfaction will last longer than it would after the purchase of a new car. The most deeply motivated people connect their dreams to a cause that is larger then themselves. The ultimate level of goal setting is when you are able to use your life in service of something greater than yourself, and in addition you are able to use your strengths and talents. This will give you the greatest fulfillment.[7]

You may not be able to change your life overnight, but you can definitely change the direction. You cannot affect your past. It is over, finished, el fin, finito. Yet many people spend too much time on shoulda-coulda-woulda. Sorry, it's over. Stop looking back. The past is what I call "dry cement." You can't change what you ate for lunch yesterday, or what you said to your boss yesterday. Learn from your mistakes and move on.

What is in front of you is all wet cement. You can mold it to work for you NOW regardless of what happened in your past.

Goal setting is a fabulous thing, yet the goal of goal setting is not necessarily the achievement of the goal. Is it great to buy the new house, get the promotion, and lose the weight? You bet it is. Yet I've seen people buy the new house only to have it burn down, get the new job, only to be downsized, and lose the weight and then gain it back. The beauty of goal setting is not only the achievement of the goal but also what you become in the process. Achieving goals gives you the confidence that you can achieve, which makes you feel like a winner. This affects all areas of your life and builds who you are at your core. Putting these principles to work for you doesn't make your life perfect, but it gives you a strong foundation on which to stand. It gives you deep roots, so to speak. The storms of life still come along, but because you have strong roots you are able to withstand the winds and the rains. When bad things happen to you, you are able to pick yourself up faster and move on.

I am not married to Stephen anymore; he is a good man, but we weren't happy in our marriage anymore. That is not to say our goals together were for naught. I learned a great deal from him in our marriage, and I am grateful for the time we had. The strength you gain from achieving goals helps you keep moving forward.

So I ask you not to be shy and to write down what you really want. If your life is fine the way it is and you don't want or need anything else for yourself, that's fine, but then why are you reading this book? You are evidently looking for something. Realize that confusion is a safe place. When you say that you're fine and you don't want anything, then you have nothing to do. You can put this book down, turn on the television, and fade into oblivion. The minute you admit that you want something, well now you have work to do. Set a goal and give it a deadline. You have to get off your butt and do something. You see, confusion may be safe, but clarity is power.[8]

Not only do I get inspired by my own goals, but by those of my friends and clients.

I met Gilda in graduate school. She was smart, goal oriented, and at the time very focused on her career and climbing the corporate ladder. On one occasion she told me that she was thinking of taking a sabbatical. She wanted to take a year off, she told me, but she wasn't sure what she was going to do. The first thing she did was purchase a few books on how to take a sabbatical. A year or so later she told me that she had saved enough money so that she didn't have to work for two years. Wow! I was impressed. "How did you do that?" I asked. "I did what the books said," she said. "I set a goal, I ate a bag lunch, drove an old car, and saved wherever I could." She then told me that she was going to spend a year studying languages in Spain, Italy, and France.

I was so impressed with this. I watched Gilda as she sold and donated most of her belongings, sublet her apartment, handled how her bills would be paid while she was away, and quit her job. She did just what she set out to do. She spent the entire year studying Spanish in Spain and Italian in Italy. She never did make it to France, but so what? She had a fabulous time, and she learned so much about herself on this journey, but none of it would have happened if she had not set the goal.

What is something you've always wanted to do? What are the excuses you tell yourself for not doing it? Gilda didn't decide on her goal and then jump. She planned for it, she educated herself, and she took baby steps.

I was so inspired by what she had accomplished that I looked at my own life again and reexamined if I was going in the direction I wanted. Travel and language are both very appealing to me, and if I want to keep them in my life on a regular basis, I am going to have to set goals that center around them. Her accomplishments gave me energy, enthusiasm, and a new outlook. That is the cool thing about goals—you can be inspired by someone else's success.

If you don't set goals, you will continue to drift along like a raft in the water. Without a goal, the raft will drift aimlessly and go with the current.

A goal without a deadline lives on forever, like when I used to say I wanted to go back for my master's degree. I talked about it for ten years, but until I gave it a deadline, it didn't come true. So set goals of all kinds, be kind to yourself, and get going.

MAKE it a habit

- Start with a simple list of what you want in the following categories: family, health, career, fun, finance, and so on.
- Type the list up, and make them as specific as possible.
- Break each goal down into steps if necessary.
- Set deadlines for completion.
- Acquire an accountability partner.

15

Habit 12: Create Affirmations for Your Goals and Dreams

"To accomplish great things, we must first dream, then visualize, then plan . . . believe . . . act!"

—Alfred Montapert[1]

Your subconscious mind acts like a tape player. It stores all the things you have learned over the years on tapes in your brain.[2] These tapes enable you to drive a stick shift, talk on the phone, and drink something at the same time without consciously thinking about it. Not that I recommend you do that. Your subconscious mind stores the program for how to drive, how to run, and how to walk. Your subconscious takes over your actions so that you can focus on other things. Your conscious mind can only do so much, and most of the time, it is your unconscious mind that is running the show. The question that I ask you now is, what tapes are stored in your mind? The golden nugget is that you can reprogram your tapes and your subconscious through affirmations. If you choose, you can rewrite the tapes and rerecord them.[3]

A woman I worked with had gone through a bad breakup almost a year and a half ago, and she told me she still cries over him everyday. "Really?" I said. I didn't know. Then she said something very telling to me. "Yes," she said. "He was the one who didn't want me. He has made a new life for himself, and he doesn't want me to be a part of it. He is happy with his new girlfriend, and he is happy that I am so sad."

I later played her conversation over in my own head, and I had a big aha moment. Now I do admit it is always easier to see someone else's problems clearer than your own, but I thought to myself, if that was the tape I was playing over and over in my head everyday, I too would be sad and crying. By saying the same sad things to herself every day, she was reactivating all the pain she felt over her breakup. What she needed was to rewrite the tapes that played in her head.

In Habit 3 I told you to visualize your tomorrow tonight, and in Habit 10 I explained the benefit of guiding your thoughts all day long. The next step is to write down statements of what you want to believe. These are called affirmations.

An affirmation is a positive statement you say about yourself written in the present tense; it is a formal declaration of something you aspire to be. For example, "I am easily and effortlessly making three sales before noon." Affirmations create what is called structural tension in your brain. When you say for the first time, "I am easily and effortlessly doing 100 regulation push-ups," the undisciplined part of your brain says, "Yeah right." At first your brain doesn't believe the words you are saying, because in the present they aren't true . . . yet. The key here is that you have to take action. You have to start doing something in the present that will lead you in the direction of your affirmation or goal. When the structural tension enters, you have to either take action toward what you want or give up the affirmation. It is said that the words "I am" are the most important words in mental programming. When your brain hears these words, it pays attention. You don't want to use the words "I will" because it implies that you may or may not get around to it in the future. "I am" is powerful and absolute and much stronger than "I will."

Just as the thoughts you have are powerful, so too are your words, and affirmations are the perfect way to reprogram your subconscious mind to work for you instead of against you. Many people tell themselves day in and day out things like, "I am fat," "I am stupid," and "I am broke," and then they wonder why this is what they have manifested in their life. If you want to know what your future is going to look like, pay attention to the thoughts in your head today and the words you say to yourself. Whatever follows the words "I am" is the direction your life is headed.

Below are some simple guidelines for creating affirmations:

1. Must be a positive statement

   (Yes) I am a nonsmoker.
   (No) I don't smoke.

2. Must be personal, about you. Start with the words "I am."

   (Yes) I am a positive person.
   (No) My significant other is a positive person.

3. Must be stated in the present tense; describe what you want as though you already have it, or as if it has already been accomplished.

   (Yes) I am enjoying my new BMW 328 convertible.
   (No) I will get a BMW.

4. Be specific: Vague affirmations produce vague results.

   (Yes) I am vacationing this May in the Cayman Islands.
   (No) I want to take a vacation.[4]

Use the space below to try your hand at writing some affirmations for yourself.

_____

_____

_____

_____

_____

_____

_____

One suggestion is to write down your affirmations on index cards, type them up, and print them out, or create a vision board (explained more in the next habit). I suggest writing an affirmation for each of the different goal areas in your life: health, relationships, career, and so on. Keep your affirmations where you can see them, read them, and say them out loud to yourself as often as you think of them. My home is filled with affirmations. I write them on index cards and hang them where I can see them.

This is where you can adjust some of your earlier tapes. Most people are really good at beating themselves up. They say things like, "I am such a klutz," "I am terrible with names," "I am so forgetful, I'd forget my head if it wasn't attached." If these are the statements people say out loud, just imagine what people are saying to themselves. You want to start giving your brain positive messages about yourself. "I am great at remembering important appointments." "I am excellent at and take joy in remembering peoples names." The reality is that your brain only believes what you tell it, and if you've been telling it what a loser you are for years, you believe it.

Some people say that affirmations are corny and it is like lying to yourself. I say it is amazing what happens when you write a lie on a card and then say it over and over to yourself over time. You eventually believe it and become what you think. Try it on, and you be the judge. The repetition and the practice of saying it to yourself consciously over and over again is what will take this new thought and change it into a permanent belief. Isn't this the way you learned your spelling words and your multiplication tables when you were a child? You repeated them over and over again. You used flash cards over and over again, until you knew them by heart.

Once you have the affirmations down, it is always a good idea to add visualization to the mix (Habit 3). Visualization is the process of closing your eyes and creating a scene in your mind. It is your ability to create a mental image. A few people have told me that they can't do this because they are not creative. I will tell you this is exactly what you are doing when you worry. You are visualizing the worst, a bad scenario, or something in your mind that causes you to worry. For example, if you have a fear of flying, the fear is in your mind, and your brain visualizes the worst that can happen the minute you buckle your seat belt. But if you would just stay in the present moment, you would realize that the plane is fine and people are talking, reading, and watching movies. On some level, you are already using visualization, so why not take that energy that you use so well for worry and turn it around? Instead of visualizing what you don't want, why don't you visualize what you do want and combine it with empowering affirmations?

Affirm and visualize yourself achieving your goals, fulfilling your dreams, and making a difference on the planet. You see, your mind does not know the difference between something that is imagined and something that is real. That is why nightmares upset us. Our brain doesn't know the difference. You may be in deep sleep and then all of a sudden you are awaken by a bad dream. As your brain wakes up and comes into focus, you realize that it was only a dream, but the emotions you felt in your body were real. Try it on—what have you got to lose?

Go back and look at the goals you have written for yourself and then write affirmations that support your goals. For example, "I am enjoying taking my new boat out on the lake every weekend." Try it on for 30 days and you will be amazed at your results.

MAKE it a habit

- Review your goals and turn what you want into an "I am" statement of affirmation.
- Write or type up your affirmations and put them where you will see them each day.
- Say your affirmations out loud to yourself a few times each day.

16

Habit 13: Create Visual Affirmations, Posters, and Reminders

"Good business leaders create a vision, articulate the vision, passionately own the vision, and relentlessly drive it to completion."

—Jack Welch[1]

Every day your brain is flooded with images and messages. You can't go on the Internet without pop-up dialogs springing into view, drive down the freeway without reading billboards, or watch television without being interrupted by scrolling advertisements and tickers. Why do you think advertisers do this? They do it to get our attention. Studies have proven that the more you are exposed to something, the more you approve of it and the more familiar it becomes to you. This is called the "mere exposure effect" or "the familiarity principle."[2]

The more you are exposed to something, the more embedded in your brain it becomes. I suggest you flood your brain with images that you want. Put your surroundings to work for you. I am a visual person, so I use photos, magazine pictures, and quotes that I hang in locations where I will see them as I go through my day. I keep small dry-erase boards on my kitchen counter and in my bathroom where I write down positive thoughts, quotes, and affirmations. You can put quotes, photos, and messages to yourself everywhere and anywhere: in your bedroom, on your refrigerator, in your weekly planner, on the banner message on your cell phone, and even in your car.

The trick here is to constantly change and update the messages. If you don't, they will become part of the background and something that you don't see anymore. Keep them fresh, new, and alive. Inspirational quotes, photos, and affirmations help to cheer you up when things aren't going your way. They push you to keep going forward, and they make you think in a new and different way. When you look at something that appeals to you, you feel good. It can be compared to the endorphins that are released while running; it elicits a pleasurable feeling in your body. By filling your surroundings with positive images, you are continually triggering the good emotions and energy that keep your spirits lifted.

A vision board is another way to capture your goals and visions. Simply put, a vision board is a visual representation of your goals, desires, and affirmations. This can be done on a simple piece of poster board where you cut out images from photos and magazines of what you want and arrange them in a collage. You can cut out headlines that capture your dreams or create your own written messages. The purpose of the vision board is that it activates a feeling inside you, which activates the goal-seeking mechanism in your brain, which helps you achieve what you want.

Every year I create a vision board. As I mentioned earlier, as a child I would always make a collage on my closet door. When I was young, the collage had no conscious purpose, other than the fact that it made me feel good. I liked looking at the images and pretty pictures. As an adult, I am now conscious of the power of these images and how they motivate and get embedded in my brain. I now know that my brain is a goal-seeking device, and if I feed it images of victory and success, that is what I will achieve. So throughout the year I keep a folder in my in-box on my desk ,and as I see images in magazines that speak to me I rip them out and put them in my folder. When the time is right, I sit down with the images I have collected, and then I cut out some more. I cut out words and phrases that mean something to me and inspire me. I take out some poster board and my glue stick and go to work.

I cut out pictures of athletic, strong, and beautiful women of all colors. I cut out pictures of places I would like to visit, people flying in the sleeper seats on an airplane, and scenery pictures that simply move me. I cut out poems and pictures of happy couples, confident business-women, dancing women, people leaping for joy, and colorful flowers. I cut out people participating in sports I love or would like to try: golf, skiing, biking, scuba diving, and surfing.

I happily glue them to my poster board, and in the end I am very pleased with my creation. I even include photos of myself within my col-lage. I am like a proud schoolgirl and hang my new vision board on the wall of my office. Every time I look at it, I am reminded of my strength and what is possible in my life. It brings me such a joyful feeling.

Here is my vision board:

After my divorce, I wrote in my journal on numerous occasions about the type of man I wanted to meet. I wrote down the qualities I was looking for, that I wanted him to be athletic and own his own business. I also wrote that I wanted him to be from another country. In my mind I was hoping to meet someone from Italy or Spain since that is my background. In addition to writing in my journal, I took an 8½ x 11-inch picture frame and made a collage of what I was looking for. In it I placed a large picture of a couple skiing, a smaller picture of two people biking, and another of two people enjoying an intimate moment in the sea. I put this on my kitchen counter and went on with my life.

I honestly don't remember the timing of all of this, but when I met Gary in Vail, Colorado, while I was on a ski trip, it all came together. He skied, biked, and scuba dove, and he even owned his own business. The only difference was that he was from the United Kingdom. I laughed to myself when I realized that I never specified the country. We fell in love and are very happy today.

I don't want you to think this is hocus-pocus and that what you want can be achieved by simply hanging up a picture, but the combination of all the habits I am writing about will lead you to success. You can't just read one book, write one affirmation, or hang one picture on the wall. The power comes from overlapping all these habits. When you stay focused and you practice repetition, then you will see results. You have to take action, do the work, put yourself out there, and take a chance.

Everything starts coming together when your habits build upon each other. These are some of the ones we have covered so far that overlap:

1. Write down your goals.
2. Create affirmations for your goals.
3. Visualize your goals and create a visual representation through quotes or pictures and hang them in your home and office.
4. Take actions toward your goals.

I was asked recently to make vision boards with a Brownie and Girl Scout troop. I explained what a vision board was in simple terms and let the girls go to work. What happened was very interesting, but not surprising. The younger Brownies, who were seven to nine years old, dove right in and had a much easier time making their board. The Girl Scouts, who were about thirteen to fifteen, were much more discerning. They were self-conscious of what the other girls would think or say about the pictures they chose, so they chose carefully. Some of them barely cut out anything at all, while the younger girls were deep into the project. At what age did you start worrying about fitting in with your peers? That was clearly at work here. My goal for you is that in doing this exercise, you get in touch with your true goals and visions for your life and that you don't let the voices and opinions of others drown out what you want.

What I want you to realize is that everything has energy, from the people who live in your home to the chair you are sitting on. These visual images, pictures, and quotes have a positive energy. The kind of energy you want in your life. Make it a priority to surround yourself with things that make you feel good, alive, and bursting with fun. You will be glad you did.

MAKE it a habit

- Make a folder for yourself in which you add magazine pictures and quotes that speak to you.
- Buy some small dry-erase boards and place them in strategic places in your home. Fill them with inspirational quotes and messages to yourself.
- Invite some friends over and create your own vision boards.

17

Habit 14: Start a Mastermind Group

"A candle loses none of its light by lighting another candle."

—Unknown wise person

So now you have written your goals down, you wrote down some affirmations, you have visual reminders in your sight, and you still find yourself not completing your goals. What else can you do? You have to take action. Having your goals written down and hanging on a board over your desk is a start, but you must take the necessary steps to reach your goals. I find that what helps give goals a boost is an accountability partner. This is a person or a group of people who hold you accountable. I suggest you start a mastermind group. Mastermind groups date back to ancient Greek philosophers, such as Socrates. They were a lively group of individuals who came together to share ideas and insights. I first read about mastermind groups in Napoleon Hill's book *Think and Grow Rich* (written in 1937)[1]. I started my first mastermind group in 1998 and have enjoyed more success than I ever dreamed was possible for myself as a result of my group.

Mastermind groups work because you have an accountability partner (or partners), and you have to report in on your progress to another human being each week. A mastermind group is a group of like-minded positive individuals who come together to share and aid in each other's growth and success.

I have had many different forms of mastermind groups over the years, and people have come and gone from my original group. What I have learned is that when people have someone hold them accountable to take steps toward their goals, most achieve what they want much faster. Over the years, the people in my mastermind group have gotten themselves out of debt, started new businesses, sold homes, completed their doctorate, and made time to be more active in their children's lives. Our goals were all different, but the one thing we had in common was our desire to fulfill them.

Here are some instructions on how to start a group of your own.

Step One: Select the right people.

Ideally a group should consist of five to seven people who are willing to commit to work together personally and professionally, but a mastermind can consist of just two people. Make sure to select positive ,powerful people for your mastermind group. You want people who have a positive outlook on life and will give your meetings energy and vitality. You don't want a bunch of negative people in this group or it will turn out to be a complaining session. People may think you are a little crazy at first when you start calling and asking them to join, but if you persevere, you will find magnificent people willing to join and share in the success.

Step Two: Everyone must make the commitment.

A mastermind group is designed as a long-term support system. Everyone must be willing to make the commitment to the success of themselves and others for the long term. This is not meant for people who don't have the time to commit. If you are committed to the process, you are expected to attend all meetings and be an active participant.

Step Three: Determine the details of your meeting.

Decide how often you would like to meet. Decide where you will meet and for how long. My mastermind group meets for a few hours once a month. We meet at one of two locations that are quiet and where we will not be interrupted. With all the technology these days, you could probably meet via Skype or some other medium, but I have never tried that as of yet. If you can meet more than twice a month, that is even better.

Step Four: Decide on your format.

How do you want to format your meeting? What do you want to talk about? You want this time to be valuable and not turn into a coffee hour. A basic format to follow is to give each person an allotted amount of time to speak. In this time they will highlight one to two accomplishments since your last meeting, state what goals they want to achieve before your next meeting, and ask for guidance on any roadblocks or pitfalls that impede them from accomplishing what they want. When one person is speaking, the rest should be silent unless called upon. All attention is on the speaker. The magic of a mastermind is that you now have all these brains helping you work through your roadblocks. It is truly a fascinating experience.

On accomplishments: Big and small accomplishments should be shared. Taking the time to celebrate the small everyday accomplishments will make way for big accomplishments.

Guidelines for Mastermind Group Goal Setting:

1. Must be specific.
2. Must be measurable by you and another person.
3. Must be important to YOU (can't be something someone else wants you to do).
4. Must have a deadline for completion.

Timekeeper: It is a good idea to elect someone to be the timekeeper at each meeting. It is very easy to go off on tangents, and then the person who speaks last ends up rushing through their piece. I find that a simple kitchen timer or cell phone timer works great, and the bell keeps everyone honest without feeling guilty for cutting someone off.

Step Five: Accountability.

Decide how you will track your progress from month to month. You can each track your own progress or you may want one person to take minutes each month. The key here is to keep each other accountable. If you don't keep your fellow masterminders accountable, that lets you off the hook with your goals and defeats the whole purpose. Remember, the purpose of this group is to achieve, to live the life of your dreams, and to not cop out. In a supportive way, hold each other's feet to the fire; you'll be glad you did.

I wish you nothing but great success in starting your own mastermind group. You deserve the best, but only you can claim it for yourself. Please write me and let me know the magic you have worked through the ancient art of the mastermind group.

MAKE it a habit

- Select five to seven positive goal-oriented people to start your mastermind.
- Meet at least once a month.
- Hold each other accountable to achieving goals.

18

Habit 15: Be Grateful and Celebrate Your Wins

"The more you praise and celebrate your life, the more there is in life to celebrate."

—Oprah Winfrey[1]

When I was in my early forties it suddenly dawned on me that everything I loved about myself was due to my parents. I guess you could say I always gave them credit, but I had been spending a lot more time with them, and this was a huge aha moment for me. I was truly touched by them and how our relationship grew, so I decided to write them a letter. Here is what I said:

July 15, 2003
Dear Mom & Dad,

It was such a pleasure spending the weekend with you. I had a terrific time and was reminded once again how truly blessed I am. You are the most giving, thoughtful, supportive, loving parents anyone could ever ask for. I am often overcome with such emotion, love and adoration for you. Yet it is so difficult to put into words all the glorious feelings I have for you. One thing I do realize now that I am older is that all of the things that I have loved about myself are the traits I have gotten from you. You have taught me so much over the years and I am continually amazed at how much I still have to learn. I know you love me as much as I. I just wanted to express how overwhelmed with love and respect I am for you. So much at times, it brings tears to my eyes.

I am blessed. I am loved. I love you.

Love,
Michele

What I didn't expect was for them to frame it and hang it in the hallway of their home. That is how much my words meant to them, and it has stuck with me. They already knew I loved them and was grateful to them, but the gift of expressing it to them in a letter made us all feel fabulous. Who could you write a letter of gratitude to, and what are you waiting for?

I am not a religious person, but I am deeply spiritual and I do believe in God. I have always felt a close relationship with God and I've prayed and talked to him in my own way almost daily. One of the ways I am able to express my gratitude for all I have been blessed with is to write "Letters to God" in my journal. It is usually a combination of my thanking him for my bounty and asking for wisdom and guidance. Here is an excerpt from my journal:

> 2/20/11
> Good morning God,
>
> Thank you for all the blessings in my life. I have been riding this wave of energy and happiness. I have been brimming with new ideas and I have been taking action to make them come true. I feel a lightness and a rightness in my spirit. I feel that I am at such a good place in my journey. I feel strong and confident and I thank you.
>
> Please show me where to direct all this energy in a peaceful and purposeful way. I know I am on the crest of a wave of good fortune. My soul is ready. I just sometimes feel like I have so many fabulous ideas and projects and not enough time to focus and accomplish them. Dear Lord, please use my life and guide my steps.
>
> Show me who I need to call or reach out to, to get the business and the projects that make my heart sing. Help me be loving and gentle with the people in my life who are on a different path than I. I am ready to take my spirit on this journey and I realize that not everyone in my circle is ready to take these steps. Please bless me with your wisdom. I trust you. I am ready. I am able and I am grateful.
>
> Love,
> Michele

Life will never give you more if you are not grateful for what you have. I read a great quote once that said if we were all able to throw our problems in a pile and we got to see everyone else's problems, we would quickly grab ours back. HA! That still makes me laugh out loud. Ain't that the truth.

I often think of my friend David, who died of a brain tumor at only 37 years old. He was always so full of life and love. Whenever I had a problem, he was always there to give me a new perspective on it. Sometimes I find myself wishing he were here to talk to about things, and sometimes I long for his encouragement or his advice. I think, gosh, David would love to be here to help me with this. And then I think, gosh, David would love to have my problems right now.

When you are grateful, you are focusing on what you have, not on what you don't have. You are in a sense amplifying the good in your life. This helps you to cope when things aren't going so well, and it boosts your self-esteem and self-worth. When you purposefully focus on what you are grateful for you will find yourself experiencing more positive emotions, which will then begin to multiply. The same is true if you dwell on your misfortune. You will find more things to be unhappy about. It is your choice.

In *The How of Happiness* by Sonja Lyubomirsky, her scientific research found, "People who are consistently grateful have been found to be relatively happier, more energetic, and more hopeful and to report experiencing more frequent positive emotions."[2]

Be grateful for everything, even your problems. Be grateful for the chair you are sitting on, the sun on your face, the tree in your yard. Realize that everything you have has been made by someone else: the car you drive, the clothes you wear, the toothbrush you use, and so on. Be grateful for the many people that make your life possible. Gratefulness is an energy like anything else. When you respect and are thankful for what you have in your life ,that energy repays you greatly.

One way to amplify what you are grateful for is to keep a "Grateful Journal." Years ago I heard Oprah speak about it, and I started one for myself. Every morning or evening you literally write down three things that you are grateful for. In the beginning you write down obvious things, for example you write that you are grateful for your family, your health, your career, and things like that. These are the common things that most people are grateful for, but over time you will want to challenge yourself to be more creative and expansive in your thinking. This activity would get boring if you wrote down the same things day in and day out. This is how you expand your ability to see what is right in front of you and be grateful for all of it. For example, you can write down that you are grateful for noticing a bird singing in a tree, or the way the clouds roll across the sky, or the smile you received from a friendly stranger. It is amazing what will happen to the way you see the world if you leave your house everyday looking for three new things to be grateful for. According to positive psychology, this is one of the easiest ways to raise your happiness rating.

Take the time to celebrate your wins, small and large. Most people take the time to celebrate the large milestones in their life—milestone birthdays, anniversaries, graduations, and things like that. What I want you to take notice of are the small milestones you hit everyday.

Too often we easily beat ourselves up for things that didn't go our way or for things that we didn't accomplish, but rarely do we celebrate the little milestones. We take them for granted, and when people tell us we are doing great work, we say we are just doing our job. In an effort to build your core, everything counts. Give yourself credit, big and small, and give yourself a well-deserved and often overlooked pat on the back. Writing it down just cements it and really makes you realize that you have much more to be grateful for than you may have previously thought. Whenever I am going through a hard time in my life and I find myself saying, "Why me?" I take out my journal and start a list of all the things I am grateful for. In the scheme of things, once I do this, whatever was making me sad usually doesn't seem so bad anymore. If you can't think of a single thing to be grateful for, put your hand to your chest, feel your heart beating, and be grateful for that.

Another way to celebrate your wins and be grateful is to create a brag book or an appreciation folder. This is a place that you store any commendation letters, cards, or emails you receive from others. You can put pictures of yourself that you are proud of, certificates of achievement, and newspaper articles and such into this folder/book. It is as easy as taking a folder out of your desk and labeling it "Appreciation Folder." Any time you receive a card, email, or letter from someone telling you that you did a good job, print it out and put it in this folder. People often send you an email thanking you for this or that, or a card, and you should put them in your folder. Once you start to save them all in one place, they will accumulate and really start to have power. Over time your folder will grow fat with good words all directed at you. Whenever you find yourself having a bad day, I encourage you to open your folder and read all the nice things other people have said about you. This will remind you that you are a good and worthy person, and that you are simply having a bad day. This too shall pass. It will remind you that you have so much to offer the world.

Once your folder is overflowing with cards, letters, and articles, you can start a brag book. I got this idea from a colleague who was going on a job interview, and instead of taking just his resume, he had a three-ring binder filled with all his accomplishments. The book included certificates of achievement, sample projects he had worked on, commendation letters, and more. Each of these items was placed in a page protector in the binder, and it looked impressive. I thought, "What a great idea." Most people would show up to an interview with a resume, but this was far better.

Go through your folder and select the letters, articles, and photos that you want to put in a brag book. The sense of accomplishment you will gain by doing this project will be well worth your effort. All of the things you are proud of and that made you feel good will now be nicely arranged in a binder and all in one place. With today's technology, you can scan your documents into your computer and design something really creative and unique. So often you don't realize all the great things you've accomplished because they are spread out over time, but having them all together in one place is powerful.

If creating a brag book overwhelms you, simply keep a list of your successes. For many years I have kept a list of business and personal successes that fueled me to keep striving and achieving. Whenever I feel that I am not achieving a goal as fast as I would like, I take out a piece of paper and write down all the small, seemingly insignificant steps I have taken to achieve that goal. Doing this makes me feel accomplished and gives me the motivation to keep going. It reminds me that nothing is built overnight, but rather one step at a time.

Another suggestion a friend gave me that I love and use often is to take a grateful walk. Sometimes when I am stressed, I put on my walking shoes and hit the trail. While I am walking I start to go over all of the things I am grateful for. If no one is around, I even say them out loud. Once I start taking inventory of all that I have in my life, whatever was bothering me seems insignificant in comparison.

MAKE it a habit

- Keep a grateful log.
- Take a grateful walk.
- Write a grateful letter.
- Take some time at night before bed, or early in the morning, to count your blessings.

19

Habit 16: Let Life Touch You

"You would never know happiness if you never experienced sadness."

—Unknown wise person

You have been given emotions for a reason . . . to feel them. Happiness, sadness, tenderness, joy, frustration, anger, grief, and all the others. Many people are out of touch with their emotions because they are living only in their head. We don't let ourselves truly feel all of our emotions on either side of the spectrum, may they be happy or sad. It has been estimated through research on emotional intelligence that 36 percent of people cannot identify what they are feeling.[1] We have been taught to suppress our emotions or take a pill the minute we don't feel well. When our neck aches or we get a headache, instead of looking at what has been going on in our life that may have caused us this pain, we take a pill. Many people are simply out of touch with themselves. Yes, there is a place for medication, and yes, some people are clinically depressed and require such help, but if you aren't one of those people, it may help to connect with the true source of your discomfort.

We don't like feeling sad or frustrated, so we push those feelings away and ignore them. Most people feel they deserve to be happy all the time, and they don't like dealing with uncomfortable emotions. I say, let yourself feel them. If you cut yourself off from your negative emotions, you may avoid pain, but in the long run, you avoid happiness, joy, and delight.

When we feel joy, we are afraid to really let it out for fear we will look silly. We have this elated feeling on the inside, yet we mask our excitement on the outside. We show that we are happy, but we hold back. We are adults, after all—"What would others think of us if we behaved like a five year old?" we worry. "Who cares?" I say.

Think about what a child is like when they are experiencing joy. How they can't keep the smile from their face or the excitement out of their eyes or the squeals of delight from their lips. Let yourself do the same. Let yourself go and dive deep into joy. When you see someone and you are happy to see them, let your face light up. Not only will this make you feel good, but think of how fabulous the other person will feel as well.

When you have experienced a serious loss, take time to grieve. Feel the hurt, the anger, and the pain. Let yourself feel it to the depths of who you are. Only then will you be able to start working your way back to joy. If you mask it, bury it, and don't deal with it, it will resurface when you least expect it. You have to move through pain and not try to go around it. Don't judge your emotions—just accept them and move on.

It has been said that people of earlier generations expected life to be hard, so when bad times came upon them, they gritted their teeth and moved forward. The more recent generations are of the school of thought that life should be easy, and when difficulties come their way, they fall into the victim "Why me?" mode. The minute something hurts or doesn't feel right, we don't investigate the problem, we medicate ourselves. We believe pain is something to run from and avoid.

When you are sad, be sad. Sit with it. Feel it. Most important, accept it. If you feel like crying, cry. While going through my separation, I cried so much and for what seemed like a very long time. The smallest of things would trigger an old memory or an emotion, and my tears would flow. I wondered if it would ever stop. Then one day a song came on that at one time would have made me bawl, but I was able to listen to it and feel fine. I've learned that if you let all your tears out and feel your feelings, eventually you will stop crying.

Once you accept an emotion, you are then able to move through it. If you are sad about something and your sadness is filled with anger about the situation, you will not be able to move forward constructively. If you can't believe this or that has happened and you are looking to place blame, you will remain stuck in your negative emotions. The reality of all of this is that bad things happen sometimes. That is part of life. At times in your life, you will feel sadness, frustration, and hurt, and there is nothing wrong with that. This philosophy has helped me to be peaceful in the midst of negative events. I am able to remain grounded much more of the time, and I don't get sucked in to everyone else's drama, and that feels great. Now, being peaceful doesn't mean that everything and everyone is peaceful around you; it simply means that from your core, from the depths of you, you are peaceful.

If you want to laugh, laugh. If you feel like crying, cry. How can you know your highs if you never allow yourself to feel your lows?

Accept the reality that your life is lived in the present moment and this moment is all you have. Accept whatever the moment is giving you. Once you accept your situation, you will be at peace with what is. You will find that the more in touch with your emotions you are and the more you let yourself feel them, the sooner you can get back to feeling good when you've had a bad day. Allow yourself to feel bad for a period. Don't allow yourself to wallow in pity. There is a big difference. When you are having a bad day, feeling down, or in a rut, the one thing that works wonders is journaling (I talk about this in Habit 21).

When your fight or flight gets engaged and you find yourself ruminating in negative emotional patterns, pay attention. Tune into your body and feel your breath shorten and your chest tighten. You know this isn't what you want to be feeling, and you especially know that it isn't good for you. Instead of beating yourself up because you know better, take a deep breath and be kind to yourself. Force yourself to stop what you are doing and feel what is going on in your body. Find a quiet place to sit still. Close your eyes and focus your attention on your breathing, which will bring you back to the present moment. Do a quick five-to-ten minute meditation to feel what you are feeling and release the emotions that are causing you stress. Sit calmly and take a series of deep breaths. With each inhalation, think of whatever is bothering you and causing you stress, and with each exhalation, imagine releasing it from your body. Thank your body and your mind for working to keep you safe, but then assure yourself that this is an emotion you don't need right now. Feel it, thank it, and then let it go. This works almost every time, and it will amaze you at how much better you feel. Ahhhhhhh . . .

When you are filled with passion and enthusiasm, ride the wave. Passion is nature's way of telling you that you are on the right path. Motivation is when you set a goal and move toward it, but inspiration is when the goal sets you and you are being pulled toward it. Have you ever been so inspired that you knew deep down in your soul that you were doing the right thing? Have you ever been so passionate about a subject that you couldn't stop learning about it? Pay attention to the times that you are overwhelmed with passion. What is it that lights you up? Can you imagine what life would be like if you did everything with your whole heart? I think it would be pretty awesome. But just like you should take the time to feel a hurtful emotion and acknowledge it, you should feed your passion when it comes. Write about it, talk about it, have a conversation with yourself about it. The root of the word "inspire" means "to breathe into."[2] Breathing is something you do naturally every day. When you are inspired, it is your true calling speaking to you.

I say let it out. Sing out loud, dance in the street, and hug a stranger if it feels right. Don't hold your joy back. Squeeze every drop out of all your experiences.

MAKE it a habit

- Tune into your emotions and identify how they make your body feel.
- Tell yourself that all your emotions are good and meant to help you on your journey.
- Stop what you are doing and take three deep breaths to honor whatever it is you are feeling.

20

Habit 17: Pay Attention to the NOW

"Don't let yesterday take up too much of today."

—Will Rogers[1]

This is the yin and yang of life, or the paradox, as they say: Goals are great for keeping you focused and helping you to achieve future successes that require planning and commitment. The key is to not be attached to your goals. To not live for the goal, and stay in the present, is a goal in itself. Remember the gift in goal setting is not achieving the goal but who you become in the process. It is the process of being. Living for now and realizing that now is all you have.

Think about how many times you have driven yourself to work and never noticed the sky or your surroundings. We actually become numb to our surroundings if we are living in our head and not in the moment. Our minds are racing all over the place, thinking of past events and what will happen in the future, and we don't see what is right in front of us. What will keep you connected to the present moment is your breath. Make it a habit to take three deep breaths at various times during your day. During the deep breath, use your senses to focus on what your eyes see, what your ears hear, what you smell, and what your body feels. The deep breath forces you to center yourself and come back to the present moment and to take in your surroundings. This works when someone else is talking to you as well. It is so easy to not focus on what a person is saying and to get caught up in thinking about what you want to say next. The deep breaths remind you to give the person talking your full attention and to stay focused and present.

Practice for yourself a few times a day. Stop whatever you are doing and take three deep breaths. Then ask yourself how you feel. What do you see, smell, and hear? Just let yourself be with whatever comes up for you.

Be present and feel. Joy happens right now in the moment, but you have to make yourself aware to experience it.

Studies have shown that lucky people are more relaxed, and they live in the present moment. Because they are in the present moment and relaxed, they are actually more open and receptive to what is going on around them, which leaves them open to more opportunities and chance encounters than someone who is stressed out and rushing. They are more apt to start a conversation with someone, or see a ten dollar bill on the ground, than three people that just rushed by.[2] When you are rushing and living in your head, you miss out on what is happening right in front of you. Quality requires attention. If you tune into your surroundings more often, you will begin to see beauty everywhere in the smallest of things— to stand under a star-filled sky and really see it and breathe it in. That is powerful. That is present moment awareness.

Unfortunately our left brain works against us. The right brain lives in the moment, right here and right now, but our left brain lives in the past or the future. It is constantly organizing events, times, dates, and so on so they make sense and have an order. The constant chatter in our heads is primarily about what has happened in the past or what is going to happen in the future. Very rarely is it about what is happening right now. Herein lies the great mastery that people have been working to achieve for as long as time. Living in the present moment.

Doing one thing at a time will help you be in the moment. When you are eating a meal, don't do anything else. Don't be talking on the phone, watching television, or typing on your computer. Just sit and eat. Smell your meal, feel the texture of the food on your tongue, and taste each bite. Slowing down will help you enjoy and savor the experience.

This is why I like exercising and being in nature so much—because it is at those times that I lose myself and I find it easy to be in the present moment. I can have a hundred thoughts running through my mind, but if I go for a walk or a workout, I find that they all melt away, and when I am done I am in a much calmer place.

Bringing your awareness to the present moment will also help you in building positive habits, which is what this entire book is dedicated to. I know when I am not living in the present moment I can easily scarf down an entire bag of potato chips unconsciously. If I were present, I would have paid attention to how the chips felt in my stomach and I would have stopped eating them sooner before I emptied the entire bag. Any time you bring your attention to what you are doing, you will find that it will be easier to make a better, more empowering choice, and your negative habits won't be repeated as often.

MAKE it a habit

- Tune into your senses a few times a day.
- Make it a daily habit to take a deep breath and look up at the sky every time you go outside.
- Set the alarm on your cell phone to ring at various times during the day. When it does, stop what you are doing and take three deep breaths.
- When you are doing something, don't do anything else—focus on what you are doing alone. Don't multitask. Do one thing at a time and give it your full attention.

21

Habit 18: Only Let into Your Life the Things You Want to Influence You

"Everything counts."

—Unknown wise person

My girlfriends and I used to have a joke when we were younger and looking to lose weight. We used to say that the broken cookies didn't count. We would then proceed to drop (oops) a bag of cookies on the floor so that they would break. We would tear into the bag and happily eat all of the broken cookies because we told ourselves that they didn't count. Now, do the broken cookies count? YES! Everything counts! Everything you let into your world has an affect on you. Never forget that.

Now with that said, I want you to be honest and answer the questions below. I want you to think of three people whom you feel fantastic around. They are a joy to be around, and when you leave them, you feel good about yourself.

Then write down the names of three people who drain all the life from you. When you see their name on your caller ID, you automatically cringe. When you leave them, you are tired and drained. There are two types of people in the world: ones who give you energy and leave you feeling fabulous, and ones who take your energy and leave you depleted.

Then do the same for the books you are reading, the television you watch, and the music you listen to. Don't skip this part. It may seem insignificant to write these things down, but I assure you it is not. I call this the flashlight exercise. It is like you are shining a flashlight on your life to take a closer look at what is working and what isn't.

Write down the names of three positive people in your life:

1._____

2._____

3._____

Write down the initials of three negative people in your life:

1._____

2._____

3._____

Write down the titles of three excellent books you have read:

1._____

2._____

3._____

Write down the titles of three books you plan to read:

1._____

2._____

3._____

Write down the title of your favorite television programs:

1._____

2._____

3._____

Write down the names of three of your favorite songs:

1._____

2._____

3._____

Now ask yourself the following questions:

1. Who are you around?
2. What are they doing to you?
3. Where do they have you going?
4. Do the people you spend your time with bring you up or hold you back?

I distinctly remember being a participant in a seminar when the seminar leader asked that last question. I took a mental inventory of the people I was spending my time with that evening and found that I could be doing a better job at this. There were some people in my life who were extremely negative and living in drama. These weren't horrible people. Most were sincere, good, hardworking people, but I would definitely not define them as positive, uplifting people. Other people in my life were also good, decent people, but I just didn't have that much in common with them anymore.

I made a decision right then and there to limit my time with them. I didn't call them up and say, "Hey, I made myself a 'positive people list,' and you didn't make the cut." I simply stopped being available every Saturday night for dinner, lunch at work, and things like that. Over time we just drifted away. I still see them occasionally, and it is okay to have occasional friends if they don't take up too much of your time.

Now at this point of my live seminars, someone inevitably says, what if it's my boss, spouse, and so on. Let me address this right now.

First the boss: You will never reach your full potential if you are working for someone who is negative and not supportive. You may think it doesn't affect you, but it does. This isn't a book about communications or managing upward, but if you're in this situation, I would buy a book on that topic immediately. Remember the only person you control in this situation is yourself, and you teach people how to treat you. It may surprise you how if you change the way you interact with your boss, he or she may become easier to work with. If putting those suggestions to work doesn't improve your situation, I would start to look for another job. Does that seem radical to you? I don't think so. You have so much to offer the world, and so much you can become. Why would you limit yourself by working for someone who doesn't appreciate you? Why would you subject yourself to dragging yourself out of bed every morning to go unwillingly to a place where you are not thriving and growing? Call me crazy, but if you find yourself a boss who is receptive and appreciative, you will be a lot more productive and happier.

Now the heavier question: What if it is your spouse, mother, brother, or close friend? The same advice applies. Ouch! I know, that sucks, but it's the truth. Every person carries with them what I call "an energy." Can you deal with it? I'm sure you can—that's not the question here. The question is, do they lift you up and help you get everything you want out of life or do they bring you down? You may think that you can handle being in a relationship with someone who is negative or doesn't share your values, but in the long run this will wear on you and they will bring you down with them. As the saying goes, if you want to know what a person is like, look at the people they spend their time with.

You cannot escape negativity or negative people all together. In fact, you wouldn't know positive if there wasn't negative. The key here is to consciously control your environment and limit your association. Make a conscious decision to seek out positive and empowering people. You will be surprised at where they show up in your life. I had been working at the same company for over nine years when I made a conscious decision to seek out positive and empowering people. As soon as I made that decision, I started meeting people who worked only a few cube rows away from me. They were there all the time, but I wasn't looking for them. Remove toxic people from your life, or limit time spent with them, and expand your circle of association.

Who are the people in your own life who are draining you? They are like psychic vampires sucking all the life out of you. Ask yourself, "Are these good, sincere people whom I love and can accept for who they are, and yet limit my time with them, or are they negative people who can easily be removed from my life?" Only you know the truth.

As far as television, books, and music go, I am not asking you to shoot your television. Just be conscious of what you are watching. Television gives you many opportunities to watch programs that inspire, motivate, or educate. The question is, you are watching those types of programs? You may want to be up to date on all the latest news, but honestly that takes about fifteen minutes. You have to be smarter than the newscasters. The same bad news is played over and over, hour after hour. They report it, give their opinions on it, get other people's opinions, and then deliberate over it. Most of what they are reporting is out of your control and doesn't effect you directly, and you can't change it. Put your life and your time to better use.

Whenever you turn the television on, ask yourself if what you are watching is adding something to your life. It is okay to want to simply be entertained sometimes, but there is a difference between quality entertainment and garbage. There is a lot of garbage out there, and you need to know the difference. In the end you are often better off reaching for a book or going to bed early when there is nothing of value to watch.

The next question is, when was the last time you read something of quality? Newspapers don't count. Sorry. Studies have shown that 58 percent of adults never touch a book after they leave high school.[1] I recall reading an article once that stated that major bookstores have reported that they believe only one out of ten books they sell are actually read. We look all smart when we have these books on our coffee table or on our shelves, but are we actually reading them? One of my friends started dating a new woman, and he was all excited about how much they had in common. He actually said to me, "She has read a lot of the same books I own." He owned the books, but he never read them.

Take inventory of your life and of the people and things you let influence you and take up your time. Never forget that, like the broken cookies, everything counts.

MAKE it a habit

- Consciously look to meet and spend your time with positive people.
- Limit your time spent with people who deplete you of energy.
- Be selective of what television programs you watch, books you read, and music you listen to.

22

Habit 19: Motivate with Music

"Music washes away from the soul the dust of everyday life."

—Berthold Auerbach[1]

This habit could be considered a continuation of the previous habit, but since music is so much a part of my life, I have decided it deserved its own space. Music has played a strong part in my family. I grew up in a household where music was on all the time and with a father who loved his rock 'n' roll. My parents encouraged us to turn up the volume, dance, and sing. While my dad did poke a bit of fun at us for not knowing how to carry a tune, he was always the one singing the loudest. I have such good memories of the times when we would all be hanging around with family and friends and the next thing you know we are having a sing-along. We knew the words to every song, and singing together made me so joyful. As an adult I carry this memory with me and consciously choose the music I listen to.

I want you to think back to a time you just left a great musical concert or movie that moved you, lifted you, and made you feel good. Or remember a time you were driving in your car on a warm sunny day, you had all the windows open, and your favorite song came on the radio. You immediately felt happy, and maybe you began singing at the top of your lungs. Think back to how good you felt. Now what I am asking you to do is to consciously create that atmosphere on a regular basis. Don't wait for your favorite song to come on the radio by chance; create moments for yourself that bring you to that place of good feelings with music. With technology it is so simple. You never have to go anywhere without your music. Whenever you need a boost or want to hear a song to lift you up, it can be right by your side and ready to help you at a moment's notice.

When you want to lift your spirits, music is your secret weapon. Some people pop a pill when they are down, but I suggest you pop in your favorite artist. When you hear the words to your favorite song, your physiology will transform and you will feel great. Music has the power to touch you on a deep level and can literally change your mood. When you listen to music, you stimulate your body to create serotonin, which is the hormone that makes you feel happy. Studies have shown that music makes you feel better and elevates your mood even after you have stopped listening.[2]

Create different playlists for yourself with the goal of evoking a certain mood. Many people will make a playlist that pumps them up and motivates them through a workout, but you can also have a playlist that simply makes you smile, one that makes you feel lucky, another strong, and another brilliant. Why not make a playlist that sets the tone for your day? Have a playlist for when you need to unwind and relax. Music is a powerful force in your life, and you have the means to combine the songs you love together in one place. The cumulative effect of that will show in your demeanor.

I want you to become purposeful about what you listen to on a regular basis and not leave this to chance. It is important that you pay attention to how certain songs make you feel. Sometimes a song can activate a painful memory, either by its words or by what was going on in your life at the time it was released.[3] When I was going through my divorce, the Eagles came out with a new album. The only problem was that most of the songs were about relationships gone bad, and I was not in the proper state to listen to that type of song. It was an awesome album, but at the time, I had to take a pass. It has been said that people who listen to romantic songs after a breakup recover ten times slower than those who don't.

This has a lot to do with the habit of affirmation. If you are singing over and over to yourself a song that states, "I'm a fool and losing you is the worst thing I ever did," that is how you are programming your mind. Instead, find a song that affirms what you want to feel. I have a playlist I made when I was going through my divorce that I entitled, "Stay Strong Girl." I filled it with uplifting, positive songs about strength, courage, and wisdom because that was the message I wanted to feed myself. Listening to powerful songs of affirmation can reprogram your mind and turn what you're singing into an empowering belief.

Many years ago I shared this tip with a client. He agreed and went on with his life. A few weeks later he came to me and said, "Wow, what a revelation." Once he really started to pay attention to what he was listening to, he realized that it was very negative. What he once thought was music that stood for something and had a message, he now realized was negative and was bringing him down. He made a decision right then and there to alter the type of music he chose to listen to. What a cool aha moment for him.

As for my family, music still connects us. On a recent ten-hour car trip on the way to our family vacation, my brother had made a special playlist of songs he thought we would all enjoy. We put the playlist on in my car and sang away, still remembering all the words and having a virtual concert in my car. It made the time pass quickly, and we took turns listening to each other's playlists and sharing songs we thought the other would appreciate.

Think about what type of music moves you, or what artists get you tapping your feet and feeling better about life. Make it a point to put them in your life on a more regular basis. It's your playlist, it's for your ears only, so why not put music to work for you?

MAKE it a habit

- Select an emotion such as joyful, grateful, or relaxed and create a playlist filled with songs that elicit that emotion.
- Keep your playlists on your iPod, phone, or portable device.
- Instead of watching the news in the morning, motivate yourself with music.

23

Habit 20: Spend Time in Self-Reflection

*"Only in quiet waters things mirror themselves undistorted.
Only in a quiet mind is adequate perception of the world."*

—Hans Margolius[1]

One of the best ways to grow and learn about yourself is to spend time in self-reflection. Contemplate your life and think about where you have been, what you have learned, what you still need to learn, and where you are going. When was the last time you stopped and took some time to reflect on your life? What areas are working? What areas could use improvement? Many people are so busy doing, running, and going that they never take the time to do this. Once they graduate, achieve the diploma, and get the job, or whatever, they never look back.

I have given so many seminars in corporations where, after the seminar, someone approaches me and tells me that they really aren't living the life they were meant to live. I've heard everything: I fell into the family business because it was expected of me; I got a job working in the financial industry because I want to make a lot of money even though I hate the work; my mother always thought I should do "blank," and so I did; it wasn't what I wanted. These people have all lost their way and have probably never done any real soul-searching or spent time in self-reflection. I mentioned "Picket Fence Syndrome" earlier, and we have all been influenced by it in some shape or form, but let me explain it a little more here. Some of us bought the dream and others rebelled, but we've all heard of it.

It goes something like this: "In order to fit in with society, you should get a college degree, get a job, get married, buy a home, have 2.1 children ,and live happily ever after." Have you ever heard that one? My parents never really said these words to me exactly, but the messages were loud and clear. The messages you received may have been another version, but still they were there. As if by osmosis, we all know what society expects of us, what our parents expect of us, and so on.

There are so many things out there influencing you that you really must take the time to hear the beat of your own heart and to listen to the words deep in your own soul. You must stop and listen to those little voices that tug at your heart. Are you going too fast to pay attention? It is so easy to occupy your mind with other things that you never spend any time alone with your thoughts. So many of my clients get up in the morning, spend all day at their job, and then go home to their families, televisions, and computers, and never take any time to reflect. Noise, distractions, and technology have made it difficult to find time to be with yourself, but reflection is the best gift you can give yourself. As Socrates warned, the unexamined life is not worth living.

The purpose of self-reflection is to examine your life and your experiences. By actively examining areas of your life, you can then improve upon what isn't working for you and make changes. You take control over your life and make conscious choices. The habit I am suggesting you develop is to spend time in self-reflection on a regular basis. This is best done alone and in a quiet environment free of distractions. I believe the most successful people plan time for self-reflection. Look at all different areas of your life and ask yourself a series of questions. When you ask and reflect on the right questions, you are able to connect with your inner self and you will grow. If you have never done this before, the answers might not come quickly, but I guarantee that if you are gentle with yourself, they will come.

Ask yourself what you want your life here to be about? What do you want to be remembered for? What are the top priorities in your life? Do you make time for them? Just sit, be still, and listen quietly and calmly for your answers. Write down your answers in your journal. You will find that writing takes fuzzy ideas and clarifies them. It articulates what you are feeling into something more concrete and actionable.

In order to get started on your own I have organized a list of questions for you to start with. Find a quiet and peaceful place to sit and read over the list and listen to your body. Which questions tug at you? Start there. These are meant to be answered slowly and over time and then repeated again as you grow, change, and evolve.

1. Who are you?

2. Where are you going?

3. What are the most important things to you?

4. What makes your heart sing?

5. What is your greatest unfulfilled desire?

6. What stops you from attaining it?

7. If you had a million dollars, what would you do?

8. What is your ideal career?

9. What is your biggest fear?

10. What could you do right now to start living a life you love?

I was giving a class many years ago, and I had the class write down the answers to some of these questions. A man raised his hand and said, "I'm 42 years old, and no one has ever asked me these questions before." I told him to be grateful that someone is asking him now. Many of us are so busy running, doing, and accomplishing that we never take a step back long enough to ask if we are going in the right direction.

I once heard another trainer tell this story, and it stuck with me.

Pretend you are sitting in the back of a cab, headed for a meeting on the other side of town. The driver is speeding fast, but you aren't paying much attention. You are in the back seat busy reading emails on your phone when you look up and realize the cab is going in the wrong direction. You immediately yell up to the cabbie, "Hey! You are going the wrong way."

The cab driver responds, "Maybe, but we are making great time."[2]

The moral of the story is that it doesn't matter how fast you are going somewhere if you are going the wrong way. Our culture sends a message to go fast, to be busy, and to fill in your calendar with meetings, lists, and things to do. Unfortunately, being busy does not equal being productive, and it definitely doesn't equal being fulfilled.

In Daniel Pink's book *A Whole New Mind*, he explains the human need for fulfillment. It is not enough to have financial success, career success, and a white picket fence. Once you find those things, you then seek self-fulfillment. It is what Maslow's hierarchy of needs refers to as "self-actualization." Pink explains how if you drive through an affluent neighborhood, you will see yoga, meditation, and spiritual centers because people are looking for meaning.

Stuff won't fill you up. The storage business in the United States, Pink claims, is a 22 billion dollar industry, bigger than the motion picture business. As a culture we have accumulated so much stuff, thinking it would make us happy, that we now have to pay for a storage unit to keep it all in.[3] You have to fill yourself up, and it is much easier when you know what makes up your happiness and fulfillment.

Self-reflection will uncover what this is for you and help you to connect to yourself on a deeper level than you ever expected. Seek out books, classes, and people that will challenge you to examine your life and the direction you are going. Simply answering the question "Who are you?" at different stages in your life will challenge you to reflect. It is much better to take time during your life to look over how far you have come and to contemplate where it is you want to go than to just keep running and then wake up one day to find yourself at an advanced age and feel that you missed out on some of the things you had always wanted to do.

My best advice here is to work through the process of self-reflection. I can't give you the answers, but I can guarantee that if you give this the proper attention, the answers will come to you. You already have the answers, you just have to slow down long enough to tune in to them.

MAKE it a habit

- Create a once-a-year ritual for yourself to reflect over the past year and ask yourself the questions provided in this chapter.
- Seek out people, classes, and books that will force you to reflect.
- Journal your answers to the questions in this chapter.

24

Habit 21: Journal

"Journal writing is a voyage to the interior."

—Christina Baldwin[1]

In September 2006, when my marriage was on the rocks, I decided to take a trip by myself to Spain. I had traveled by myself for business trips many times, so I assumed I'd be fine. Vacations, I learned quickly, are a little more fun when shared and a lot more fun when you are fluent in the language.

My language skills were worse than I thought, and my confidence with what little Spanish I did know was gone. I was scared to open my mouth. I wandered around lost and lonely, wondering, "What did you do, Michele? The first time you decide to take a vacation by yourself, you had to pick a place where you aren't fluent in the language. What are you, crazy?"

I am a talker, a communicator, and here I was, scared to open my mouth. The reality that I had lost my voice hit me like a ton of bricks. I had lost my voice literally and figuratively. I had lost my voice in my marriage, I had lost my voice in my life, and now I had lost my voice for real.

This is where my journal came in. I took it everywhere with me. Not only did it give me an outlet for my voice, but it also helped me clarify my feelings about my life. I titled it "The Michele Buenafuente Phillips Find Your Voice Tour 2006." I wrote out all my feelings, all my thoughts, the funny stories that happened on my trip, and the mishaps I experienced due to the language barrier. Writing gave me an outlet, clarity, and comfort.

When I finally did leave my marriage, I had forgotten how loneliness felt. I hadn't been on my own, ever. Again, my journal became my constant companion. Being positive and motivating was what I did for a living. People took my classes to feel good about themselves, and here I was feeling hopeless. I was afraid to put those dark feelings down on paper. I was afraid to give them life, but they wouldn't go away. On the nights I would lie in bed and the lonely feelings would overtake me, wrap me up, and torture me, I would reach for my journal. Writing calmed my nerves and brought me peace. It built me up and made me strong again.

I want to share with you an entry from one on my loneliest moments. My purpose in sharing it is to highlight the power of reflecting on your thoughts and fears through journaling, and to show you that I too have fears, and how journaling made me stronger, more focused, and more sure of who I am.

Journal Entry October 7, 2007—Lonely Little Girl

That lonely little girl came to visit today. As I was driving home, I just started to cry and was overwhelmed with sadness. What am I afraid of? I'm afraid I will be left all alone in this world. I'm afraid that everyone can smell my loneliness. I'm sad that there isn't that one special person who cares about me. Who cares what I am doing and where I am. Isn't this what you wanted? Freedom? Freedom to do whatever you wanted? Now that is what you have. Stay calm, Michele, and know that this too shall pass. You are strong, beautiful and intelligent, and you can get through this.

The simple act of writing my thoughts and feelings down helped to center me. Journal writing is an ancient tradition, and many successful people in history have kept a journal. It is said that Leonardo da Vinci never went anywhere without his journal.[2]

Today I am in a much more confident and happy place. I still fill volumes of journals, but now not only are they a place for me to capture my worries and fears, but they are also creative outlets for brainstorming ideas, capturing funny and touching moments, taking notes on passages in books, and recording significant lessons in my life. I travel with my journal everywhere. It has become a habit that I am in love with. I truly believe that you can't journal for an extended period of time without experiencing a breakthrough, achieving clarity, or having an aha moment.

If you are one of those people who doesn't believe in journaling for whatever reason, that's cool. All I ask is that you don't skip this section. Research has shown that writing forces you to organize the thoughts that were once bouncing around in your head. When you do this you gain a better sense of control over what is happening to you, and, as a result, you are able to deal with your challenges more effectively. It has also been proven that writing about the experiences in your life—whether they are positive or negative—strengthens your mental and physical health. Writing forces you to select your words carefully, and when you do this, your energy will follow your words. When you are able to release your feelings of hurt, anger, and fear onto paper, you also release the feelings in your body, and as a result your feel calmer and more centered.[3]

Writing about positive events helps you relive the good feelings they brought you. And when you write about things you are passionate about, you invite more passion into your life. It is as if writing about it breathes more passion and excitement into whatever it is you are pursuing. So whether you are sorting out your feelings, brainstorming new ideas, or writing about a lesson you learned, journaling can be beneficial. It helps you clarify your thoughts and know yourself on a deeper level, and it can reduce stress.

To begin this habit, buy a journal that speaks to you and feels good in your hands. Spend at least twenty minutes as many times a week as you can writing whatever comes to your mind. Don't worry about spelling and grammar—just write what you are thinking. If you need help starting, look back to the questions I gave you under the self-reflection section and journal your answers to those questions. I guarantee this process will help you to know yourself better, and it will become a friend to you, as it is to me. Don't think about it like a diary. A diary to me is something that you are required to write in everyday to account for the events in your life. A journal is different. One day you could takes notes on a passage in a book that moved you, and another day you could work through a problem you are having with your mother-in-law.

I recently had dinner with an executive I had coached for two years. He admitted to me that when I first gave him a journal, he wasn't thrilled with the idea. However, he completed his assignments and carried his journal with him on all his flights. He now gives journals out to people who report to him, and he explains to them the power of organizing their thoughts and knowing themselves through journaling. He has experienced the power of journaling firsthand and now wants to share it with others. As with all the other habits I'm suggesting, try it on for yourself.

MAKE it a habit

- Buy a nice journal that feels good in your hands.
- Set aside twenty minutes a few times a week to start writing whatever comes into your mind.
- Write down your answers to the self-reflection questions in the previous habit.

25

Habit 22: Take Responsibility for Your Reactions

"When we are no longer able to change the situation—we are challenged to change ourselves."

—Victor E. Frankl[1]

For me, learning to take responsibility for everything in my life was the most powerful thing I have ever done. Before I learned to take responsibility for the conditions of my life, I often let my emotions rule me. I was a reactive person instead of a proactive person and when the events of my life didn't go my way, my reaction was to scream, yell, and blame outside circumstances.

Growing up I developed a very bad temper. I thought my temper was part of my DNA, and that it was simply who I was. My father had a bad temper, my brother had a bad temper, and so did I. We are passionate people, I told myself.

One of my most embarrassing moments where my temper got the best of me was an occasion when I had a fight with Stephen. I left in anger and was speeding up a street that was long and straight. My temper was on fire and this was the perfect place to speed like a demon. The only problem was that the road was about to end and I was still speeding. I had to make a left or a right. In my cloud of anger I went flying straight through the intersection, over the curb and into the woods. Someone was watching over me that night, because I made it out fine and lived to tell about it. Needless to say, I am not proud of this event, but I am sharing my story for a reason.

The next day when I went back to where I went off the road, my skid marks were long, dark, perfectly straight, and visible on the pavement.

A few days later I was driving with my girlfriend and we passed the skid marks. She scoffed, "What moron did this? Didn't they know the road was ending?" I just agreed with her and laughed out loud, never identifying myself as the "moron." A few weeks later we were passing the same location, and again she laughed out loud, "This cracks me up, what a moron this person was." I couldn't take it anymore. "It was me!" I exclaimed, "I'm the moron!" This is only one story of how I let my emotions get the best of me. I unfortunately have many more stories I could tell.

Through my studies, I learned that while you may not have control over the emotions you feel—and each of us has approximately 27 emotions an hour[2]—what you do have complete control over is what you do with those emotions. How you react to an event literally controls your outcome. If you leave for work in the morning and hit traffic, your reaction could be to tell yourself that your day is ruined. Then the rest of the day you will be in a bad mood. Or you can tell yourself that you are determined to have a good day no matter what happens, and when you get to work you are still in a good mood. It is your reaction to the traffic that sets your course for your day, and you have 100 percent control over that.

If you want to create a better life for yourself, take responsibility for what you have created. Everything you have or don't have is a result of a decision you made. Some people don't like to hear this. It is so much easier to blame someone else for why you don't have what you want. People love to blame the government, their boss, their teacher, and my all time favorite, their mother. Now granted, as a child, choices were made for you, and you may not have had much say, but let's face the facts now, You are an adult and you have say in what you do. I will tell you that you have 100 percent control of your reactions.

The best way to illustrate this is with a formula I learned in 1997, when I went to Jack Canfield's seminar. This is a simple formula, which made a tremendous impact in my life, and one I use every day. It is simply E+R=O.

The formula says that everything in your life is an **event**. Getting out of bed this morning was an event, driving to work an event, and so on. Events are not good or bad.

The world is just out there doing its thing. You put meaning to the events based on your **reaction**, and this in turn gives you an **outcome**.

The lesson here is that if you don't like the outcomes you are getting the key is not to change the events. Most of the time you have no control over the events. What you do have control over is your reaction to the events. If you take control of your reactions, you will create better outcomes for yourself.

Here is where the RESPONSIBILITY part comes in. Notice the word, RESPONSE-ABILITY. The meaning of the word comes from your ability to respond. We control that 100 percent, but most people don't take responsibility for their reactions. It is so much easier to blame the boss, blame our parents, blame the government, and whoever else you can think of rather than take 100 percent responsibility.[3]

Now I don't know where you fall with this formula; maybe this is something that you have been practicing all your life and you have it down pat. Maybe you are similar to the way I was and you are relating to everything I've said. Maybe you are saying, "I don't have anger issues. I don't see what the point is. When the events in my life don't go my way, I don't say anything. I don't have a temper." If you don't have a temper, do you hold everything inside and let your emotions eat you up from the inside out? The two ends of the spectrum are the anger-out-of-control side, which was the side I was on, and the hold-all-your-emotions-inside side, and neither is good. Then there are all the variations in between. The habit you want to cultivate is being able to choose your reactions once your emotions are triggered to allow for a constructive reaction instead of a destructive reaction.

This formula works for everyone no matter where you fall. Whenever you find yourself frustrated or stressed, ask yourself, "What is the event that just took place?" Then ask yourself what your response to that event was. Are you getting the outcome you want? If not, your only choice is to change your response.

This is much easier in theory than it is in practice, but like anything else it is like a muscle and when you work the muscle it gets stronger and eventually becomes your habitual way of dealing with challenges. I will admit that I didn't like learning this formula and was actually quite offended to learn that I had control over my reactions. "What do you mean, I have control?!" (said in a sarcastic tone). I much preferred to blame outside circumstances and people for my destructive behavior. I would often hear myself saying, "Look what she made me do," and "He made me so angry." Through applying this formula I learned that nobody made me do anything, and that if I practiced this I was actually much more empowered than ever before.

MAKE it a habit

- Write the formula E+R=O and put it where you can see it.
- When you feel tension growing in your body, stop, step back, and ask yourself what just happened, and what is your reaction to what happened.
- Ask yourself what the outcome is that you are looking for and choose a wise response.

26

Habit 23: Become an Optimist

"A happy person is not a person with a certain set of circumstances, but rather a person with a certain set of attitudes."

—Hugh Downs[1]

I don't know if you are a glass-half-empty or -half-full type of person. I will tell you that if you are a glass-half-empty type of person you are probably right in your calculations about life and how things are going to happen. Pessimists, it seems, are more accurate. If you are a glass-half-full type of person you probably take more risks, fall down a little more often than most people, but you are having a lot of fun living life. Optimists may try something way out of their league, but they enjoy the process. Pessimists might be right more often, but optimists are more successful.

In 1998 the field of positive psychology was defined.[2] A group of researchers, scientists, and self-labeled pessimists set out to find out what was all the fuss about optimism. What they found in their research was surprising only to them. It seemed that optimists had a lot going for them. They did better in school, sports, work, and life overall. They lived happier lives; they aged better; they dealt with stress, pain, and setbacks better; and they even lived longer lives. What was it all about?[3]

This movement was led by Dr. Martin Seligman, who claims to be a pessimist. What he learned was that optimism could be learned, and if it could be learned, it could be taught.[4] Sonja Lyubomirsky writes that approximately 50 percent of a person's happiness is genetic, meaning that your parents gave it to you and there is nothing you can do about it. However, 10 percent of a person's happiness is based on circumstances (where a person lives, where they work, if they are married or not, and so on). The other 40 percent lies in our behavior: our daily intentional activities, what we do, and how we think.[5] With this said, as far as I'm concerned, 50 percent of your happiness and optimism is in your hands. This research uncovered that with a little effort, it is possible to be happier. If you practice optimism, you will feel more satisfied, and you will be more engaged with your life, find more meaning, and have higher aspirations for yourself. You will probably laugh and smile more, regardless of the circumstances of your life.

Hey, I could have told you that. But I didn't, and they did, so hats off to the team of positive psychology researchers. Therefore, happiness and optimism is a decision you make, and the effort you put into being happy is your choice. I suggest that you make the choice to be a deliberate creator in the life you live.

Author Sonja Lyubomirsky found that happy people did certain things. They had happy habits. They nurtured their relationships, they sought out new experiences and achievements, they savored life's joys, and they developed coping strategies when things went wrong. I have listed many similar ideas here, but I highly recommend reading her book, *The How of Happiness*, as well.[6]

If I asked you, what are your ultimate goals? You would respond with answers like, I want to get a promotion, start my own company, marry my soul mate, have a child, get physically fit, or travel the world. If I then asked you why, you would answer me with your reason. If I asked you why again, eventually you would tell me that you want to be happy. We are all going after the same goal, but taking different roads.

If you were going to compete in your first triathlon, you would study the training habits of triathletes. You may read a book on how to train and take some tips from them. The same thing applies to happiness. If you want to be happy, wouldn't it then be intelligent of you to find out the habits that happy people have?

Research has shown that the things we think will make us happy, really don't. Most of us are brainwashed by the media to believe that a bigger house, car, a new partner, a child, a promotion, or moving to a new location will make us happier. The reality is that the happiness that comes from any of these events usually fades away after three months.[7] Physical attractiveness has been proven to bring advantages, but it doesn't have a huge effect on happiness. Studies have shown that 54 percent of adults are "moderately mentally healthy, yet not flourishing . . . [and] actively . . . engaged."[8]

The truth is that happiness is always with you, but you have to choose happiness. When you are happy, that is your true nature and everyone benefits from you being happy. Happiness comes from the inside and it is a decision you make. It doesn't matter what the weather is, how much money you have, or if your boss is in a good mood today. You can choose to be happy no matter what is going on around you. Wherever you are you can find something to be happy about if you really want to. It is as simple as appreciating the blue of the sky, a bird outside your window, or the colors on a leaf. You just have to tune in. Happiness is everywhere if you are open to it, and there is a huge difference between searching for happiness and choosing to be happy.

The world can't make you happy, but your thoughts about the world can make you happy. What if starting right now you decided that you were going to be optimistic and happy no matter what circumstances life brings you? How would your world change? When your happiness is based on having a reason to be happy, it is out of your control and it can be taken away from you at any moment. But when you can be happy without a reason, now your happiness is a decision you have made and you have control.

So how does one become an optimist? Well, you have been learning exactly how to do that by reading this book. Each of these habits is a building block to your happiness. One of my favorite techniques for becoming more optimistic is to practice optimistic explanations.

"A pessimist sees the difficulty in every opportunity; an optimist sees the opportunity in every difficulty."

—Winston Churchill[9]

Since I rollerblade so often, I have more than one story about a fall. The following illustrates the habit of making optimistic explanations. One bright sunny day, I headed to my favorite lake to rollerblade. I was flying around feeling fabulous and enjoying my music. The lake was majestic, the cool spring air flowed through my hair, and the sun shone on my shoulders, when all of the sudden I lost my balance, tripped, and fell over my feet. I don't know how I did it, but after what seemed like a long time of stumbling along and flailing, I managed to gain my balance and save myself from falling down. My heart was racing, and I was still trying to get my bearings when the words to the song on my iPod sang out, "You rescue me, you hear my cry, you shelter me through the night."

"Wow," I thought. "This is God's way of telling me I'm going to be okay, that he has me in his hands." I kept blading, and not more than fifteen minutes later I took another tumble, and this time I wasn't so lucky. I went down onto the pavement. I wear kneepads and wrist guards, but that didn't protect my shins, thigh, and butt. Ouch! I had a big old strawberry, my skin was gone, and I was bloody mess. At the end of the day, nothing was broken except my ego. I got up and moved on. "What was God trying to tell me now?" I asked. I decided that his message was that even if I do fall, I will be able to get back up and keep going.

I ask you to pay attention to how you explain the circumstances of your life for the next 24 hours. Do you take responsibility for the circumstances of your life, or do you blame others and outside forces? When things don't go your way, is it because you are a loser, or because you are having a bad day? Is your bad luck temporary or permanent? Do you find yourself saying things like, "Look what *you* made me do."

How you explain away the events and circumstances in your life is very telling. An optimist, a glass-half-full type of person will find a positive explanation for the events of their life. Just like I did when I fell down.

An optimist believes that negative events are temporary and isolated. So my falling down was a once-in-a-blue-moon event. A pessimist describes negative events as permanent and long lasting. If a pessimist took a fall, they would tell themselves that rollerblading is not for them, so they should stop doing it. The next time something happens to you, pay attention to how you explain it, and realize that what happened has happened. You have no control over the event, but you do have a choice as to how you explain it.

This has shown up when studying depression. A clinically depressed person has a ratio of one negative thought to one positive thought, 1:1. A non-depressed person has a ratio of two positive thoughts to one negative thought, 2:1.[10] This leads me to believe that happy explanations may be hard work, but they can become a habit and the health and well-being benefits are huge. Now if you are clinically depressed or have ever suffered from depression, I advise that you seek medical attention, but if you just suffer from the blues every now and then, this is a great habit to adopt.

If two people fail a test and one is an optimist and other is a pessimist, their explanations for failing will be very different. The optimist will explain the failure due to their lack of sleep (isolated) or preparation for the test (temporary). The pessimist will say they are dumb (permanent) and always do poorly on tests (long lasting). Do you see the difference between the two explanations? The first one is temporary and isolated so in the future you will get a good night's sleep and be better prepared. You are in control. The latter explanation is permanent and long lasting and out of your control. I know I would much rather be in control than not. Start to pay attention to how you explain things in your own mind and when you catch yourself using pessimist behavior take steps to correct it.

Ask yourself the following set of questions:

1. What happened?
2. What is my explanation of what happened?
3. Does this explanation hurt or empower me?
4. If this explanation doesn't serve me, what is another way to look at it? What is an optimistic way to explain this?
5. If you can't come up with something, enlist the help of an optimist.

The more optimistic you are about explaining your challenges and the events of your life, the more confident you will be about your future. When you are confident about your future, you will take more risks, set higher goals, and put more effort into getting what you want.

MAKE it a habit

- Hang a note on your bathroom mirror reminding yourself to MAKE it a great day.
- When challenges come your way make a decision that you will deal with it in the best mood possible and apply the E+R=O formula with the outcome being happiness.
- Pay attention to your self-talk and your explanations for the course of 48 hours to determine if you are making optimistic or pessimistic explanations.
- When you find yourself making pessimistic explanations, use the questions outlined above to redirect your thinking.
- Select a role model and when you find yourself being pessimistic, ask yourself how your role model would handle the situation.

27

Habit 24: If You Are Living, Be Learning

"Here is the test to find whether your mission on earth is finished. If you're alive, it isn't."

—Richard Bach[1]

After college I went through a period in my life when I stopped learning. I got complacent for many years. I graduated, got a good job, got married, went on great vacations, I worked long hours, got good promotions, and for ten years I did nothing to improve myself intellectually. I worked on myself physically, but that was it. Ten years after college my mentor encouraged me to go back to school to earn my master's degree and I did. When I got back into learning, I came alive again. I was so excited about everything and that was when I understood the value of continuous learning. I didn't realize how stagnant I had become.

The Japanese have a single word that means to always be improving and it is called *kaizen*. It stems from the Japanese words *Kai* and *Zen*. *Kai* means change, and *zen* means good. Translation: Change is good.

I would like you to think about a time in your life when you were learning something new, and I'm sure you would agree with me. When we strive for something that is important to us, once dormant forces wake up and we feel alive. In order to learn something new, you have to be willing to be the fool to eventually become the expert. What I mean is that whenever you learn a new skill, you have to be all right with looking foolish at first, and with being the novice.

When was the last time you improved yourself? When was the last time you took a class for you, improved a skill, or learned something new? So often I find that no one is getting in the way of your success but you. Many people graduate from college, earn their formal education, get a job, and then never take another class in their life. Oh, they may take a required computer or safety class here or there, but they never crack another book or work to improve themselves in any way.

When you don't continue to learn and grow, you fear you are becoming obsolete. If you are insecure or fearful that your talents, skills, or expertise isn't enough, you will give into workaholism. You will sacrifice what is important, your health or your family, in an effort to give more to your job, your career, your boss. When you are afraid to take a day off because you may be replaced, you are in a seriously bad space. How do you take control of that? I call it remaining "employable." If you continue to work on yourself on a regular basis, grow your skills and talents, you will continue to be employable. If you are part of a large corporation and you lose your job as part of a downsizing effort, you are employable somewhere else. If your talents, skills, and expertise aren't given the proper attention, payment, and accolades you deserve in your current company, another company would gladly have you. Or if, like in my case, you work for yourself, the more on top of your game you are, the more valuable you are to those who want to hire you. Either way you win.

In my coaching practice I see all kinds of people, and the most successful ones know there is always more to learn. They are open and allow themselves to be vulnerable and to be the student. I recently fired a client that was stagnant and full of excuses. He claimed he was too old to learn anything new (42), that he was fine the way he was (in a job he didn't want), and that he didn't believe the things that successful people did would work for him. After many months of working really hard to engage him in learning, I finally decided that it was a waste of both of our time. What he didn't realize is that we are never standing still. If you aren't working to grow and improve yourself, someone else is, and in reality you are sliding backwards. It takes effort to grow.

Successful people keep striving, learning, and stretching. If you think about the most talented people in any field, they spend their days practicing, stretching, and improving. They never reach a point where they stop learning and growing. We can all take a lesson from them. If all you do is improve yourself in some small way each day, over time you will achieve mastery.

Just like with all my other habits, I suggest you pay attention to the subjects that excite you and start there. I know when I pick up a book that speaks to my passion, my heart beats a little faster, my brain waits in anticipation, and my soul rejoices over the lessons and the learning I am taking in. Learning and acquiring new skills and knowledge is really exciting and fulfilling. You feel good about yourself, your confidence gets a boost, and everybody benefits from the new and improved you.

In Tony Hsieh's book, *Delivering Happiness*, he talks about the power of 1 percent. What if every day you worked to improve yourself in some way only 1 percent? If you had $100 in the bank and every day it earned 1 percent interest, you would have $3,778.34 by the end of the year. That is a big payoff for a small investment, wouldn't you say?[2]

MAKE it a habit

- Make a list of things you've always wanted to learn (speak Spanish, cook, garden, play the guitar, learn how to dance).
- Read a book on your subject.
- Sign up for a class.
- Go to the library.

28

Habit 25: Go Outside

"An early morning walk is a blessing for the whole day."

—Henry David Thoreau[1]

My advice is to make dating the earth a habit. I have said for years that I am having a love affair with the ocean. Even on the coldest of days I will make my way down to the ocean's shore to have a heart to heart and be healed by it's wonders. The ocean and I have had many talks, winter, spring, summer, and fall.

I remember one day in the middle of the summer when I was feeling very lonely after my separation. I was lying on the beach on a gorgeous sunny day. The sky was clear and blue, the beach was crowded, full of people laughing and having a great time. And there I was lying in my beach chair, alone, having my own little pity party: wondering why my marriage broke up, what could I have done differently, why I was I alone, blah, blah, blah. Everyone around me seemed so happy and carefree, and I was just getting sadder and sadder. I felt this huge wave of anguish sweep over me, and I started to cry beneath my sunglasses. "Why me?" I cried. Then I heard this voice in my head say, "Get in the water Michele . . . now!"

My body felt heavy and weak and I didn't want to move, but the voice got louder, "GO! NOW!" I reluctantly got up and made my way through the crowds, looking down the whole time, and just praying for the moment that I could dive under the water and wash away my tears. Once in the ocean, I dove deep. The water felt so good on my body. It relaxed me. It eased me, and it miraculously washed my pain away. All of the sudden, I knew that I was going to be okay. I dove down deep, held my breath and swam as far as I could. I leaped up, I spun myself backward in a somersault and felt the ocean embrace me and settle my fears.

When was the last time you spent time outside? Driving to work doesn't count. I encourage you to fall in love with the earth. Spend some time connecting with nature. Use all your senses; see the colors, feel the earth beneath your feet, and smell the air. The number one pastime in America is watching TV, followed by going to the mall, and this makes me crazy.

If you are someone who loves the outdoors, then you don't need me to convince you. If you don't consider yourself an outside person, listen up. When was the last time you spent at least an hour of your time outside? If you are an outdoor lover, when was the last time you spent the entire day outside? I challenge you to take out your calendar right now and make a date with the earth. It could be a hike up a mountain or a simple walk down the street. If you live in a city, that's okay; just get out and get some fresh air.

Try the following exercise: Take a walk by yourself, and by that I mean leave the iPod and your cell phone at home. If you are one of those people that believes you can't leave your cell phone for an hour, I will address this in Habit #30 in an upcoming section. I want this to be an intimate moment, just you and nature. I don't want you to be distracted by talking with another person or listening to music. The purpose is to just go outside and tune into your senses.

What do you see? Is the sun out? Is it warm on your shoulders? Look at a tree. Get up close and personal and look closely at a leaf or the bark. What are the clouds doing? Are they moving? Are they light and fluffy, or slim and silky? Is the sky dark? Are the stars shining like jewels littering the sky? Really look, and see the beauty. What sounds are around you? Can you hear the leaves rustling with the breeze? Are the birds singing? What do you smell? Take a deep breath of fresh air and feel it fill your lungs. What do you feel in your body? How does the earth feel below your feet? Do you feel the breeze on your cheeks? Tune into the moment, and take it all in. If you really take in the moment, you will discover the gift and the healing properties of nature. The earth will heal you and restore your strength.

I will admit that on some days it would be much easier to stay indoors and not make the effort, but you must push yourself. You will discover the reward you gain from connecting with the earth is immeasurable. Even on cold winter days, make a pact with yourself that if the temperature is above freezing and you are dressed appropriately, there is no excuse for not going outside. A friend of mine says there is no such thing as bad weather, just bad clothing. With all the new waterproof and insulated materials, you can always be dressed properly for the conditions. Once you start moving and your body warms up, it will feel as if it is 10–20 degrees warmer than it really is. So unless you live in Alaska, you should have no excuse for not going outside.

On days when you are frustrated, worried, or have lost your focus, a simple hour outside with nature can bring everything back in perspective and ground you. Within fifteen minutes of being in nature, your blood pressure will drop, and you will feel the stress leaving your body as your heart slows down and your head clears. The issues that seemed so daunting earlier will melt away.

Being outside is also linked to happiness and it is said that people who open themselves up to nature and beauty that surrounds them are more likely to find meaning and joy in their lives. The ability to get outside and relish ordinary experiences is a gift you can give yourself any day of the week. When you go outside and open your senses up to what is happening, a shift takes place; you become fully aware and present and sacred moments are everywhere.[2]

MAKE it a habit

- Take out your calendar and make a date with the earth.
- Purchase the necessary gear and clothing; you will be glad you did.
- Leave your phone, iPod, and so on at home or at least on silent.
- Stay in the present moment and use all your senses.

29

Habit 26: Give Smiles

"Everyone smiles in the same language."

—George Carlin[1]

Many years ago I made a conscious decision to practice smiling at people. I am a born connector. What makes me happiest is connecting to people, getting to know them, and bonding on a deep meaningful level. I noticed that it was easy for me to smile at someone I knew or at someone who smiled at me first. However, to smile at a stranger, or someone I had never been formally introduced to was harder. I noticed in myself that I tended to give this half-hearted smile where I kind of grinned tight-lipped and kept my mouth closed. It was a pathetic half-smile. Why did I give such a pathetic smile? Because I was afraid that they might not smile back at me and I would look foolish. I didn't want to give them a full-on all-teeth smile and then feel stupid. I realized how silly this was, but that was my reality.

I started what I called my unscientific "smiling experiment" to practice my smiling. I wanted to be able to give people a real full-on all-teeth genuine smile. I started at the lake where I rollerbladed every morning. My goal was to smile at the people who I passed. It was awkward at first, and I noticed myself giving what I've come to name the "safer smile," the one without the teeth. What started to happen was amazing, nine out of ten people smiled back, said good morning, and were genuinely happy to engage with me. "Wow! What a concept," I thought, "and how simple." I realized that a smile was the most normal way to connect with other people.

In 2002 I was in a theater bar in Manhattan where I had just ordered two drinks. As the bartender started to make my drinks, I opened my wallet and realized I had no means to pay for them. Flustered, I wondered what to do. At that moment I looked over to the other end of the bar and recognized another bartender at the other end as a girl who runs at the lake. I motioned her over, and since I had never really had a conversation with her before I asked her if she ran at the lake? She looked in my eyes, and remarked, "Oh my word, it's the girl with the perfect smile." I laughed and told her my dilemma, she shooed me away, giving me the drinks on the house.

My challenge to you: practice your smiling for the next 48 hours. Notice if you are able to give a real authentic smile to a stranger or if you give a different version. Then notice what happens. Notice how you feel and the reactions you receive. A smile not only is a gift for the person receiving it, because let's be honest, we all gravitate toward someone who is smiling versus someone who is frowning, but it makes you feel awesome as well. A smiling person is much more attractive than a frowning person. A smile can boost your endorphins and turn an ordinary day into a fantastic day. Smiling is linked to lower stress levels, a younger looking appearance, and even boosting your immune system.[2]

A smile is a powerful tool. When someone smiles at you, it immediately says you are welcomed in their space, and that they want to interact with you. Sometimes I will be giving a seminar and I am looking out into a room of serious, non-smiling faces. Then on a break someone comes up to me and says, "This is a great class. I am really enjoying it!" I then ask that person if they could let their face know. We all laugh, but seriously if you looked at many people's faces, they don't look too happy. Make sure that your face isn't one of them.

MAKE it a habit

- Start off by smiling at the people you pass on a regular basis but don't engage with.
- Take notice of what happens and your comfort level.
- For a 48-hour period, practice smiling at one to two people you don't know every hour.

30

Habit 27: Eat from the Earth

"Don't eat anything that your great-grandmother wouldn't recognize as food."

—Michael Pollan[1]

Over the years I have read a great deal on diet and nutrition. Should you eat meat? What's the deal with carbs? Can I eat a protein with a vegetable? What about antioxidants, probiotics, and gluten? As with everything else in life, my advice to you is to keep things simple and not complicate matters. There will always be a new study or a new diet claiming this or that. My philosophy for eating is simple. Eat as much as you can in its natural state. Doughnuts don't grow on trees. It is that simple. When you eat an apple or a vegetable for example, you know you are getting some essential vitamins and nutrition. You don't need to be a doctor to know that. On the other hand, when you eat something that is processed, something that has a shelf life, comes in a box or a bag, the labeling may tell you its good for you, but if you read the ingredients you will see that most of what makes up this product was made in a laboratory somewhere. It is a combination of science, chemicals, and preservatives. Again, you don't need to be a doctor to know that the better choice would be to eat a food in its natural state. With so many products claiming to lower your cholesterol, give you unbounded energy, or protect your heart health, it can be confusing to know what is good for you and what isn't.

In his book *Food Rules*, Michael Pollan sums up his case for eating from the earth like this: "Populations that eat a so-called Western diet, generally defined as a diet consisting of processed foods and meat, lots of added fat and sugar, lots of refined grains, lots of everything except vegetables, fruits, and whole grains—invariably suffer from high rates of the so-called Western diseases: obesity, type 2 diabetes, cardiovascular disease and cancer." He goes on to say, "People who get off the Western diet see dramatic improvements in their health." This is the philosophy I have adopted, and what I love about it is that I don't need a PhD in nutrition to follow it. It doesn't require me to count calories, know the definition of the word xanthan gum (the substance in many foods used as a thickener, I just googled it) or go out and buy the latest chemically engineered so-called processed food that promises to support a healthy immune system. It only requires me to eat most of my diet from foods in their natural state. This I understand and can follow. If you are still questioning this part, let's suffice it to say I am encouraging you to eat more vegetables, fruits, nuts, and whole grains and less items that were made in a factory.[2]

As for meat, I don't eat much myself, and that is a personal choice, but If you eat meat, eat meat that was raised on a natural and healthy diet of real food. Consider the fact that if the cow you are eating was fed a poor diet of nonnutritious foods and scraps, than eventually, that is what you are eating too. Don't worry about not getting enough protein if you don't eat meat. In most cases if you are eating enough calories, you are probably eating enough protein. Protein is in everything: broccoli, beans, potatoes, and so on. It may not be as high as the amount found in meat, but it's there. If you have been living off a diet of fast food, processed foods, soda, fried foods, and pastries, your diet is deficient in much more than just protein. My advice is to shop on the perimeter of the supermarket. This is where the unprocessed and natural foods are normally found. Try to limit your intake of anything with a shelf life, and that goes for soda and beverages too. Does it grow? Is it a plant? Is it low on the food chain? Yes, an apple may have been sprayed with pesticides, but it isn't as concentrated as the cow that is injected with hormones and then eats the apple that was sprayed with pesticides. You get the picture.

Hey, I live in the same fast food world you do. I have a weakness for salty foods, chips, popcorn, and pretzels. Be conscious of your consumption. Keep nuts and healthy snack choices with you at all times, just like your cell phone. I can guarantee you that if you keep a bag of almonds in your car, it will satisfy you when a craving hits. If you don't have anything in the car, you are more likely to stop for a bag of chips or go through the drive-through. If you must have chips, buy a snack bag. That way you don't feel deprived.

Learn to read labels. You don't have to be a nutritionist to do this; you can use the following questions when you are reading a label. What are the first three ingredients? Ingredients are listed in order of their proportion in the product. The first three ingredients represent the bulk of what you are eating. It is safer to stick to ingredients you recognize. Can you pronounce all the words? Do you recognize the words? Are there five ingredients or fifty? Chances are, the less ingredients that are in a product, the better it is for you. Is the sugar content of the food hidden in the label? Many manufacturers break the sugars into multiple ingredients so that it doesn't look like there is a high content in the product. Any word with syrup, or ending in "ose" is a sugar. Pay attention to the serving size of a product. A bag of cookies may claim that one cookie is a serving size. You have to be smarter than the manufacturers. Last, the name of the product has nothing to do with its health content. Don't be fooled by products that claim to be healthy.

When you sit down to a meal aim to put color on your plate. Real food has beautiful colors: red peppers, yellow squash, green vegetables, black beans, and white onions. Think about what a plate of fast food would look like in comparison. There isn't much color represented in a burger and fries. If you use ketchup, that doesn't count as a color. Aim to fill your plate with color and you will also be packing in necessary vitamins and antioxidants.

Don't attempt to exclude any food from your diet altogether. This is why diets don't work. They deprive you. Instead of taking foods away, add foods. Don't stop eating cookies, but instead add fruit to your diet. Don't swear off soda, just add eight 8-ounce glasses of water to your day too. Over time, just keep adding the foods you know will benefit your health and then listen to your body and see how it responds.

You will find, as I did, that when you become accustomed to eating real foods from the earth your taste buds will change. You will no longer crave artificial foods as often and your taste buds will know the difference. When you bite into something that is mostly chemicals, it won't taste good to you anymore, If you are anything like me, just the sight of dark green leafy vegetables and brightly colored fruits will call to you and make you happy.

Last, spend your time with healthy people. If you spend time with people who eat fast food, then you will too. If your friends are reaching for fruit instead of chips, you will follow suit. It is really hard to work at being healthy when all of your friends are chowing down on fast food. If you don't know of any healthy people, it is time for you to start making new friends.

MAKE it a habit

- Read labels and ask yourself the questions from this chapter.
- Add fresh vegetables and color to all your meals.
- Keep healthy snacks in your car, office, and kitchen.

31

Habit 28: Connect with Your Spiritual Side

"It has been said that the laws of the material world do not apply in the presence of God-realized."

—Wayne Dyer[1]

There are many definitions of spirituality. For me it as an inner sense of knowing that something exists that is greater than myself and that I can connect with this energy. It is my experience of connectedness with myself, others, and the divine energy of the universe. It is my connection to my faith, the universe, and my God. Please don't take offense from the word "spirituality." I am not talking about religion. Each religion is a path to God, but not the only way to know God. I believe that without a faith in something bigger than yourself, your life lacks meaning and purpose.

I believe that there is an intelligence that puts the red in a cardinal's wings, controls the tides, sees to it that spring follows winter, and that the sun rises and falls each day. I believe in the goodness of all people deep in their souls. I believe that I am just a piece of a much bigger picture and that I am connected to it all and so are you. When I practice my spirituality, I connect to my divine self in a deeper way and to everything the universe has to offer.

I believe that wanting to be "God-like" is the highest form of humanity. To love with no conditions, to want the best for others, and to give more than you take is something I aspire to. I believe that when I line up my thinking with God's thinking, I am on the right path. My beliefs are strong, and they run deep. I can't prove them, nor do I wish to, but that is what faith is, isn't it?

Whatever you believe or not, my wish is that we all find love and the sacred in everyday events and moments. Research has found that most people believe in something; however, the fear of offending each other keeps us silent and afraid to talk about our beliefs, when in reality most people are craving the connection. In *A Whole New Mind*, Daniel Pink states that most CEOs define spirituality as the basic desire to find value and meaning in the workplace and one's life. He also states that employees are hungry to bring their spiritual values to the workplace, but aren't comfortable doing so.[2] In a society that is based on accumulation, climbing the ladder, and being more concerned about your outer shell than your inner, our true selves are lost. If you follow people who, according to society, "have it all" (the car, the fame, the fortune), you will often find them still searching. What is it they are searching for? Usually it is spirituality and connection with something greater than themselves. When the accumulation of things proves unfulfilling, what we seek is meaning.

Tune into your intuition, to your faith, and to the side of you that can't be proved through science and research. If we only relied on our senses, we would be missing so much. Your senses tell you that the sun revolves around the earth, and that the earth is flat. We know that is not true, but if you only rely on what is logical, you are missing out.

One way to connect to your spiritual side is to read. Books will open your mind up to a variety of ideas. Don't just buy into what you read; be discerning and you be the judge. Talk to people, go to lectures, and see what resonates with you. Spending time in silent meditation is another great way to connect with your spiritual side. You cannot grow your spirituality if you fill your time with tasks, people, and things to do. Connecting to your spirit happens when you are alone in prayer, meditation, or solitude. It is when you are by yourself that you can connect with your higher self.

I will confess to you that meditation is the one habit that eluded me for many years. Every book I read talked about its powers and how it was healing and a great way to quiet your mind and restore your health. I believed the claims, but struggled with getting myself to sit still long enough to do it. Finally I committed to sit and mediate for 20 minutes for 21 days. I took my own advice. In the beginning my mind raced, my heart raced, and I felt so uncomfortable sitting there. I kept at it. Every morning my ritual was to get out of bed, put on the coffee, and go downstairs to my living room and meditate. Over time, the beat of my heart slowed down, my mind relaxed and I found myself enjoying my morning meditations. I now sit down to meditate and I get right into the groove on most mornings and it feels so darn good. After a 15–20 minute meditation, I pour myself a cup of coffee and read at least 10–20 pages to start my day off right.

You can also connect by looking for ways to use your strengths and talents in service of something bigger than yourself. Think of the talents and strength you naturally possess and find a way to use them for the good of all mankind. This is when your life takes on true meaning and this is what so many people crave. Perhaps you can work with a charity, support a local organization, or spend time with someone who is alone. Doing this has proven to be connected with the highest levels of happiness and spirituality.[3] In Dr. Martin Seligman's book, *Authentic Happiness*, he has delved into our need to find purpose and meaning in our lives. It is a question as old as time. Why are we here? In his research he has found that the ultimate level of happiness can be found when we attach ourselves to something bigger than us. When we are able to do that, we experience a feeling of satisfaction that our life has meaning and purpose.[4]

Studies have shown that people that have a relationship with God are more peaceful and calm. Having faith helps you stay calm when things in your life go wrong. Believing in a higher being gives you comfort that you are not alone. Having faith has been proven to raise positive emotions such as hope, forgiveness, and love.[5] In partnership with God, you can do great things.

This connection to spirit provides you with a renewable source of strength, courage, and wisdom. No matter what life throws at you, if you spend time praying, being grateful, talking with God, or in nature, your strength is renewed, your confidence restored, and your mind enlightened. Many times in your life you may be confused and unsure of which way to turn, or what decision to make, and this is when I recommend that you turn your challenges over to God. Trust that God has a greater plan for your life than you could ever planned for yourself. Pray that his guidance and wisdom will be delivered to you.

Many of the previous habits I've already discussed are things you can practice daily in an effort to become more mindful, connected, and spiritual. Pay attention, be still, and work to connect to your higher levels of consciousness.

MAKE it a habit

- Spend time in silence, meditation, or prayer.
- Connect with nature.
- Listen to your intuition.

32

Habit 29: Unplug

"Technology and tools are useful and powerful when they are your servant and not your master."

—Stephen Covey[1]

Slow down; decide you are not in a hurry. Nature never rushes, yet everything happens when it should. When is the last time you made space in your day to be with yourself? Do you have boundaries around your electronic devices? *Psychologies Magazine* states that "our devices are what 62% of us turn our gazes on when we wake up. Not our partner's sleepy eyes, or our child's smile, but a screen." It goes on to say that "you and your phone eat, sleep, socialize, even holiday together."[2] Are you the master of your devices or the servant? Do you respond like Pavlov's dog at the site of a light on your device or the bleep of a text? If you responded, yes, you aren't alone.

In order to do anything well, you must give it your undivided attention. This goes for a conversation, your golf game, typing an email, or cooking dinner. In other words, if you want to do something well, you have to slow down, stop multitasking, and focus on the task at hand. In a world that is full of distractions and where multitasking is expected, you may be fearful of only doing one thing at a time, for it risks looking like you are not working hard enough. When you think you are getting more accomplished by multitasking, you are really doing only a few things poorly. Your brain literally stops giving its attention to one thing, and starts up with another, leading you to do both things poorly. This frantic brain activity can lead to added stress.

Computers, phones, and the like allow us to think we are good at multitasking. Talking on the phone while typing an email is adding stress to your brain because you are using the same part of your brain for both activities at the same time. The more time you spend multitasking, the harder it is for you to concentrate on one thing in the future, and remember what I said about quality requiring attention.

Ask yourself if you ever unplug and let yourself go without your electronics. Can you go for a walk in the woods and turn your phone off or leave it at home? Do you shut your phone off at night, or does the sound of incoming messages buzz away on your nightstand while you are trying to sleep? Have you been spending so much time with your electronics that you haven't had a real conversation with your family or gone outside to feel the wind on your face?

I'm not asking you stop; I'm just suggesting that you schedule time to be without any of your electronic devices. Start with an hour and see how long you can go. Realize that in reality, you really don't miss that much, and that many of us have created a false sense of importance, thinking that we have to respond to every request real time. Unless you are an emergency medical technician, most things can wait. Don't respond to emails at all hours of the day and night.

With all this said, I will openly admit to struggling with this at times. However, I have worked to maintain boundaries around my electronics. I always turn my phone off at night. I don't keep it on my nightstand and I plug it in to charge in another room. This way I can enjoy a good night's sleep. For all of you wondering . . . yes, I do have a house phone and the most important people in my life have the number. If a cell phone is all you have, consider putting everything on silent with the exception of phone calls. This way you aren't pulled out of a good REM sleep because of a silly text or email in the middle of the night.

As emails come into my phone, there is no sound alert. I look at it all day long anyway, and the sound alert would make me twitch. When I go to the gym, rollerblade, and so on, my phone does NOT come with me. During my morning meditation, when I am speaking, or in meetings, it is always on silent. I'm not perfect, but I am working on all of this just like you. My hope is that you look at your habits around technology and admit whether they are either helping or hurting you. Once you admit that a habit is hurting you, you then have the responsibility to do something about it.

Technology was invented to help simplify our lives and not complicate things. The question is, who rules who? Do you rule your technology or is it the other way around? A high percentage of people are slaves to their technology. They walk into work in the morning, open their email and let their incoming mail dictate their day. Be conscious of how much time you spend with technology, and then look to reduce and recover. Take baby steps and see how long you can go without your device. When you are with your family, make them a priority and realize that most other communications are just distractions from being present with the most important people in your life.

MAKE it a habit

- Turn your cell phone off at night if you have a house phone. The people who really need to reach you in the middle of the night should have that number.
- When you go to the gym, leave your phone in your locker, or better yet in your car, for the hour.
- Schedule time outside, alone, without your phone.
- Unplug from everything at least a half hour before bed.

33

Habit 30: Nurture Your Relationships

"It isn't WHAT you have in your life that counts, but WHO you have in your life that counts."

—Unknown wise person

Your family and friends are the backbone of your life. They are your cheerleaders, confidants, and your true supporters. Your happiest memories are those shared with the people in your life, and in your saddest moments, your friends and family pick you up and help you start again.

When I was going through my divorce, in an effort to not be alone, I spent a lot more time with my family and friends. On those days that were too lonely and hard to bear, I knew that my sister's house was like my own house and that her family was like my family. It was the place I could go to anytime without calling ahead and feel welcomed and loved. I had been in a relationship for so long and that meant spending every weekend as a couple. Now I was alone with lots of time on my hands, and lots of sad and lonely feelings. My parent's house became my refuge too. On the weekends, I would drive the hour and a half and spend time with them, and it was during this time I really grew close to them and got to know them better. The love and level of support my family showed me was invaluable.

As for my friends, they were there too. I remember one night after crying to a friend about how sad I was that I apologized to her. I said I was sorry to be bringing her down and that I felt like I was draining her. She didn't hesitate to tell me that I had been there for her so many times in the past that she was thrilled to be there for me now. Wow! That felt good.

How often do you consciously give away your love? How often do you let love in? Have you ever considered that having wonderful relationships equals a successful life? Today's society is so concerned about driving the right car, living in a big house, and wearing the latest designer fashions. As a result, you work long hours to earn more money, to climb the ladder, and to buy more stuff, when in the long run, all the stuff means nothing. Nobody ever asks for their big screen TV on their death bed. So what about you in your relationships? If I went out and did a survey of the people closest to you, what would they tell me? When was the last time you spoke to them? Do you know what is going on in their lives?

The more supportive relationships you have, the more energy you will have to pursue your goals. Relationships don't grow strong by accident. It takes a conscious effort. Most Americans have only two good friends, yet it has been proven that the happiest people on the planet have multiple strong relationships and a great social support.[1]

Right now I would like you to make a list of all the people in your life who depend on you: your spouse or significant other, your children, your parents, siblings, relatives, coworkers, and friends. Then add to the list the people you depend on: friends, relatives, and associates.

Now write down the date of your last focused conversation. By "focused" I mean you weren't watching television, surrounded by other people, or distracted by your email or cell phone. You were with them in the present moment. I hope it was recent. Is there someone on your list you feel is vitally important to you, yet you have invested no time with him or her recently?

Your close relationships should be treated like gold. These people know the intimate details of your life. They have heard and seen it all when it comes to your life, and they love you anyway. That is what makes them so special. They don't judge you. They have seen you at your best and picked you up off the floor at your worst. Just like you deposit money in your bank account to make it grow, you need to make deposits in your relationship to keep them healthy and strong. You have to make a conscious effort to give of yourself, your time, and your love. Don't keep score. Don't worry about who called who last. Just reach out and connect with the people in your life. In the end you all win.

I knew a woman who was so wrapped up in her career that she always cancelled on her friends at the last minute and was too busy or wouldn't get back to them when they called. After a while they gave up and stopped trying. Years later when she retired, she confessed to me that she had no friends. She told me that she spent all her waking hours with people she worked with and now that she wasn't working, she had no one. Don't let this happen to you.

In order to have friends you must be a friend. You have heard that before, but what does it mean? To start with, the best gift you can give someone is your time. You can easily send a card or an email, but the gift of your time speaks louder than anything. You must make time for the people you love.

Next you must be interested in what is going on in his or her life. It can't always be about you. You can easily go on and on about your own life, but in order to be a good friend, you need to shut up and listen as well. Pay attention to the details of their lives and what is going on for them. Ask questions and follow up with support before a big presentation, job interview, or trip. Make a special effort to reach out with a quick email or phone call wishing them luck, a great time on vacation, or whatever. Your efforts will go a long way in making a deposit in your relationship account.

Confide and share. Your best friends confide in you. Trust builds the relationship, especially between women, when we share. It is important that this confiding is not a one-way street. You have to share the details of your life in order for the bond to grow. I'm not talking about gossip. Gossip is about other people. Bonds are built when you share your own dreams and fears. You may have many acquaintances, but your real friends share themselves with you at a deeper level. They share a piece of their souls with you. Yes, we are all trying our best to look perfect and pretend that we always have it all together. But, in reality, we all have fears, things that scare us and make us cry. True friends are able to share their darker side, the not-so-pretty side, and definitely not the perfect and put-together side. That is what makes your bond so special. Small talk is fine for acquaintances, but share a piece of yourself with your true friends. I am often reminded of Eleanor Roosevelt when she said, "Great minds discuss ideas. Average minds discuss events, and small minds discuss people."[2] Nurture high quality friendships and relationships.

Don't expect your friends to be perfect, and do expect them to disappoint you sometimes. If you are good friends with someone, expect disagreements and expect hurt feelings once in a while. When two people are that close it is inevitable that you won't agree on everything and that is okay. Don't judge them too harshly, because sometimes you will cancel plans or have to disappoint them. Know the intentions of their hearts, learn to forgive, and move on. You are human and so are they. Everyone is doing the best that they can. Sometime life gets busy, but your true friends know you love them, and that doesn't mean you care for them any less. If I expected my friends to be perfect, I wouldn't have any friends.

Create rituals, and schedule time to talk, laugh, and catch up. Learn "The Happy Dance." This is a celebration dance you can do whenever something good happens to one of you. You just hold hands, jump up and down and scream like twleve-year-olds. You let the joy out and it just feels good.

Schedule sleepovers and play dates. You are never too old for a sleepover. If you can get away for a weekend or an overnight with some- one you are close to, the bonding that goes on will be priceless. I learned this from my best friend Susann. When we first met, she invited herself to sleep over at my house. I was married at the time and thought it was a bit odd, but went along. The friendship we have developed has been amaz- ing, and we continue to this day to have sleepovers at least once a month.

If you are a man, sleepovers may sound a bit silly to you but a fishing or camping trip is just as good. Going to a sporting event is something everyone can enjoy. I admit that I am not a huge sports fan, but when I go to a ball game with a friend, I get so much from the time we spend together, and I don't stress out over who wins the game.

Make a date to spend time with your parents, children, or any other close relations on a regular basis. Date night isn't something just for cou- ples. Schedule a date night with each of your children. Schedule Sunday dinner with your parents, have a standing dinner night with your best friend; you'll be glad you did.

MAKE it a habit

- List the people closest to you.
- Schedule quality time with each of them on a regular basis.
- Schedule a weekend away with someone close to you.

34

Habit 31: Have a Bad-Day Emergency Plan

"Confidence is preparation. Everything else is beyond your control."

—Richard Kline[1]

Have a plan you can execute when you find yourself emotionally hijacked or having a bad day. We all have them; we all feel bad sometimes (sad, angry and frustrated). You have been given your emotions for a reason and you shouldn't ignore them. However, I am going to suggest that you don't let one bad mood spoil your entire day. We have an expression here in the United States where we say that we got up on the wrong side of the bed. What does that even mean? That means that if one thing goes wrong first thing in the morning, you now give yourself permission to be cranky and moody all day. For what? Why would you give up your day like that?

The fact is you have approximately 27 emotions an hour.[2] Is it possible for something to go wrong first thing in the morning? Of course it is. But why would you let that affect the rest of your day? Yet this is what so many people do by plugging into their negative emotions over and over again.

When something happens in your life that your brain deems as negative, you experience a negative feeling in your body such as anger, hurt, or frustration. A real chemical is then released in your body. Neuroscience has proven that within 90 seconds after the chemical is released in your brain, it literally dissolves. If the actual chemical is gone, then why do we let things ruin our day? The problem is we keep plugging into the thought over and over and retriggering the chemical reaction in our body that makes us upset. It is a vicious cycle.[3]

The strategies I suggest you use when you want to snap yourself out of a bad mood are listed below.

1. Talk to yourself and get to the bottom of what is bothering you.
2. Talk it over with a supportive friend.
3. Journal about what is upsetting you, and nine times out of ten, it won't seem like such a big deal when you put it in perspective.

When you are having a bad day, or feeling sad or frustrated, pay attention to the feeling. Give it a voice. Just like a child, it needs to be validated. Then have a plan. Use the list of questions below to gain perspective.

What am I feeling right now?

Why am I feeling? (Insert any emotion here: angry, frustrated, sad)

Where has sulking ever gotten me?

What do I want to be feeling?

What do I have to be grateful for?

What is this going to mean to me in ten years, ten days, ten minutes?

What is the solution?

Some days the littlest of irritations can set you off: a rude person, a slow driver, or your own tardiness when you are running late is enough to turn your mood foul.

Recently, on my way to England, my day got off to a less than pleasant start. I was dressed and ready to leave when I realized I forgot to stop my mail. So I quickly ran down to the post office to take care of this. When I got to the post office, they were closed for lunch and I was forced to go to the next town to pick up a form. I live in a small town and my post office is literally run by one man. It wasn't a big deal, but I could feel my stress growing due to the fact that I had to get myself to the airport. I got the form, filled it out, and left it in my mailbox. On the way to the airport, I got behind the slowest car on the local road and hit tons of traffic on the highway, so again I could feel myself starting to get more stressed. When I got to the airport, I was told my luggage was over the weight limit and they wanted to charge me an extra $100. The woman behind the counter was less than pleasant and couldn't care less that I was already stressed and rushing. I was forced to take some things out and add them to my carry-on. Most of these events were trivial, but they seemed to be piling up, and my nerves were fraying.

When I got on the airplane, I realized that I had a window seat. I always book an aisle because I like to get up and stretch on long flights. There were none available, so I took my place at the window. Then a woman sat down in the middle seat who seems nice enough, but she is coughing her head off. "Oh great," I thought to myself, "just what I need: her germs." After takeoff, the guy in front of me practically reclined his seat into my lap, and my patience was at its end. As I took a deep breath, I asked myself the questions.

- What am I feeling? I am feeling unimportant. I am feeling like a number, like no one cares about my comfort on this plane, and that I deserve better.

- Why? Because I have not gotten what I want; an aisle seat, a healthy seatmate, and some room for my book in my lap.

- Is sulking going to help me? No, the only thing sulking does is hurt me and perpetuates my foul mood.

- What is the outcome I want? What do I want to be feeling? I want to feel important and in the end I want a peaceful flight. I am quickly reminded of another Eleanor Roosevelt quote which is, "No one can make you feel inferior without your consent."[4] Whether or not I feel important is entirely up to me, and if I want peaceful flight, I either have to take action and move my seat or accept what I have been given.

- What do I have to be grateful for? So much. My life is fabulous. I have work that I love, fabulous relationships, health, travel, and so much more. I could go on, but this line of reasoning made me realize that my little pity party was unwarranted. When I looked at what I have to be grateful for, I realized that even when one or more things appeared to be going wrong, at least a dozen things were going right. When I did this, I could focus on the many things going right, versus the one or two things going wrong.

- What will this mean in ten years, ten days or ten minutes? I didn't even need to answer that one. I was in a better place mentally and I could sit and enjoy the flight.
- What is the solution? The solution in this case was for me to let it go and enjoy the flight.

Put the event into perspective, and make this your habitual way of thinking. The more you take yourself through this series of questions, the more it will become the way you process a bad day or event. The events I listed in my example seem utterly silly to me as I read them again, but I can assure you, on that day it seemed like nothing was going my way. Other times your bad day can be triggered by some bad news, a breakup, bad weather, or a disappointment from someone you trusted.

If you have experienced the loss of a loved one, or a serious tragedy, give yourself time to feel your feelings. These experiences are very different than just having a bad day. The one thing I learned is that you have to go through your feelings; you can't ignore them or go around them. You may be able to ignore them for a while, but they will resurface when you least expect it.

I then think of something that brings me joy. I recall all the things I have in my life, and pray for God's grace to point me in the right direction. I talk to myself and tell myself to get over the pity party, move on, and live joyfully.

If you need to dial a lifeline, call up a friend who will remind you just how special you are and how good your life is. "A friend is someone who knows the song in your heart and can sing it back to you when you have forgotten the words."[5]

I have a clear memory of the morning I was driving down the West Side Highway, on my way to three separate prospective client meetings. I needed to be at the top of my game. My confidence needed to be up, and unfortunately, it wasn't. The events of the last 48 hours were not good: things weren't going my way and I was feeling horrible. I knew my energy was low, and I needed to change my perspective quick. I phoned up a friend I knew would tell me what I needed to hear and put everything back in perspective.

I explained my dilemma to him and that I was having a very bad week, but needed to be on top of my game. In seconds he started telling me how much of an impact I made on him and how meeting me changed the trajectory of his life. He told me how I inspired him to do things he never might have done. He told me that I light up the lives of everyone I touch. With tears filling my eyes, I knew I was going to be just fine.

Another clever suggestion is to have all of your close friends and relatives write down what they would say to encourage you on your worst day and then seal each one in a separate envelope. Whenever you are having a bad day, you can just reach for one of those envelopes and read words of encouragement from your friends. I had a friend do this for me on my birthday one year and I thought it was brilliant!

Get out in nature and lose yourself in the trees, in the clouds, in each person's face, and realize that you are never alone. Affirm that you are in the right place at the right time, and that everything is happening perfectly. Say a prayer, ask for wisdom, and then let it go.

I have heard that just the anticipation of going to watch a funny movie, read an inspirational book, or talk with a positive friend can raise your endorphins. It makes sense to me. And don't forget how music and journaling can impact your mood.

Expect your bad day or mood to be temporary, look for the lesson, trust that the challenges you are facing will pass, and take constructive steps to prevent ill fortune in the future. If you have a plan, a movie to watch, a friend to call, or the series of questions to set you back on track, then you can be guaranteed that your bad mood won't last and you'll be back on track in no time.

MAKE it a habit

- Write down the questions and use them when necessary.
- Know which of your friends will be able to pick you up when necessary and give them your support and encouragement.
- Go outside and connect with nature.
- Watch an uplifting movie, listen to songs of affirmation, or read a book that inspires you.

35

Habit 32: Use Your God-Given Talents as Much as Possible

"When I stand before God at the end of my life, I would hope that I would not have a single bit of talent left, and I could say, 'I used everything you gave me.'"

—Erma Bombeck[1]

Wow, I wish someone told me this quote sooner. I am blessed to have found my path and make a living using my strengths, but it took me some time. If I think back to when I was a child, I was always a ham. I loved to dress up and put on a performance. I would always get my cousins involved and we would dress up and make up some kind of skit, dance, or song to perform for the adults.

My friend and I often talk about how we love being around little girls before they become self-conscious; when they still believe they are beautiful, invincible, and can do anything. I look at my nine-year-old niece now and see that unconquerable spirit in her. On her birthday when she received a picture frame, she asked me to guess whose picture she was going to put in the frame. I guessed her mother or her dog. Wrong! She informed me she was going to put a picture of herself in the frame. I should have known. Ha!

I think of how I was when I was that little girl and my passion was talking it up and performing. Yet I was always getting in trouble for my social ways. My nanny told me that I talked too loud and too fast. My father sang the fifties song to me, "You talk too much." When I was in junior high school, I was always assigned by my teachers to sit by myself. If I was sitting with other people in class, I was always talking during their lessons, and that didn't go over well.

I graduated college with a Bachelor's of Communication Arts. I chose that major because of my love for getting up and speaking in front of groups. I made Dean's list three out of four years. During college, I took an internship at the local TV cable station and before long I was cohosting the local magazine format show for the county, "Eye on Rockland." I was having a ball being in front of the camera, but once I graduated I thought it was time to get a "real" job. The unspoken rule of society told me that it was time to stop having fun and work for a living. I knew that I loved to speak, but I didn't have any idea how to make a career out of it, so for the next nine years I went to work for a big corporation. I was good at my job, but I wasn't using my core strengths or talents.

Then at the end of 1996, my company merged with another company and my position was eliminated. I was left with no choice but to take a position in the training and development department. Once I got in that classroom, I was like a duck to water. I learned that I truly had a knack for inspiring people and making them believe in themselves. This is where I was meant to be. For the first time in my life, I felt at home. I was using my strengths every day, and it felt great. After I facilitated a workshop, I felt so fulfilled inside, and the beauty was all the people who attended also felt fulfilled. This is what I was meant to do, and for the first time in my life I heard the calling. In 1998 I started a consulting company, I went back to school for my master's degree, and I have never looked back.

My talents were clear and strong since I was a young girl, yet I didn't trust myself enough to pursue them. I didn't explore my options. I just followed the crowd and got a job to pay my bills.

What are your gifts and strengths? Whatever they are, make sure you share them with the world somehow. It doesn't have to be your actual profession. I understand the need to pay the bills. It doesn't even have to be a giant gesture. It can be something simple like reading to children once a month, making beautiful flower arrangements for your friends and family, or making beautiful paintings. At the end of the day, let your talents and your gifts shine.

So ask yourself, "What have I always wanted to try?" What is it that holds you back? Has someone told you that you can't, you're not good enough, or that your idea is not realistic? People will often tell you that you can't do something because they can't do it. You have been given your talents to share, and that is the best gift you can give. If you aren't sure what your talents are, take a moment to think of the compliments that people have given you over the years. Think back over the moments and accomplishments that you are most proud of. I know you are talented beyond measure—we all are—yet not all of us have been given the chance to nurture and grow our talents.

Follow your energy—everything you want is down stream. Go with the energy—follow where your passion leads you, and see what happens. As I have said in earlier chapters, pay attention to what comes naturally and easy to you but not to others. That is where your gifts lie.

MAKE it a habit

- Identify your talents and strengths.
- Take a class to improve yourself in your area of strength.
- Commit to using your talents in the world in some small way.

36

Habit 33: Do Something Kind

*"Ask yourself: Have you been kind today? Make kindness your
daily modus operandi and change your world."*

—Annie Lennox[1]

When you think about it, every single thing you have in your life was made by someone else. The clothes you wear, the computer you type on, the chair you sit on, and so on. Even the car you drive, the roads you drive upon, and the language you speak are all gifts from others. When you really think about this it blows your mind. The question is, what then do you give in return? You could give money to charity, or volunteer your time now and again, but I have found what doesn't cost you a dime or take a lot of time is giving kindness. You can choose to give kindness to everyone you meet. It is as simple as giving a smile to a stranger or a compliment to a person you admire. These small seemingly insignificant acts of kindness carry with them so much power.

I was asked to speak at a conference once to a group of people who were unemployed. I was asked to give them hope. After I spoke, this woman approached me at the podium and I didn't recognize her in her business suit, but she said to me. "You pass me every morning at Rockland Lake." She said, "You look at me, you flash a smile, you say good morning, and you make my day." Wow, how nice was that to hear. But more importantly, I never knew how much my simple good morning meant to her. It didn't cost me anything, and I just left a little happiness in my wake.

It can be as simple as holding the door for someone, letting them get in front of you in line, or allowing them into the traffic line. You may find yourself getting annoyed when you consciously complete an act of kindness that is not recognized. For example, I've seen people hold the door open for a stranger, and if the person doesn't say thank you, the person doing the good deed grumbles an annoyed "thank you" under their breath. This is defeating your purpose. Your goal when giving kindness is to give just for the sake of giving, without expecting anything in return.

This past birthday I took my commitment to kindness one step further. I was recently asked to serve on the board of an organization called Walk 4 Good. Their purpose is to inspire others to practice kindness, and I encourage you to check them out at www.walk4good.org. A woman who knows that I serve on that board forwarded a link to me about something called Thebirthdayproject.com. On her 38th birthday, Robin Bomar and her family completed 38 acts of kindness. I was so moved by both of these organizations that I decided to dedicate the month of November, my birth month, to acts of kindness. My goal was to complete an act of kindness each day of the month and then post it on Facebook and encourage others to do the same.

Here is a sampling of some of the things I did:

- Bought sandwiches and gave them to utility workers on the street.
- Bought a bouquet of flowers at the supermarket and handed them to the woman behind me on line.
- Went to a bookstore and hid scratch-off lottery tickets inside random books.
- Scattered change in a playground for children to find.
- Waited in the long gas lines, post-hurricane Sandy, for the woman who works at a store I shop in.
- Bought a bag of chips from a vending machine and left it for the next person.
- Offered to take pictures for people on the top of the Empire State Building.
- Wrote out inspirational messages in cards and left them on random windshields in a parking lot.

By the end of the month I will admit I was running out of ideas and I said so on Facebook. People were wonderful and started completing acts of kindness on their own and posting them on my page to tell me they were doing it so that I could take a day off. Another friend posted that instead of watching me have all the fun that she too would do 30 days of kindness. It was contagious and that was what I was hoping. I believe that when you see someone do something nice it warms your heart, and makes you want to do something nice too.

Another friend suggested that I visit an old age facility. I agreed on one condition: she would come with me. We met at a home one afternoon and had the nicest time talking with Anna, Nettie, and Josephine. We learned about where they grew up, their children, and their families. It was so fulfilling for both them and us. Being kind serves you and the person you are being kind to and its value is priceless.

I will admit that making the commitment to post a kind deed every day for 30 days put some pressure on me and exhausted me at times. My suggestion is to be purposefully spontaneous. Keep an open mind and look for opportunities to practice kindness and be ready when you see an opening.

I'm sure you have been burned at some point in your life; we all have. You extended your good will to someone and it wasn't returned. You said a friendly hello to someone, and they grunted a response or you put yourselves out on a limb and nobody helped you out. As a result you may have retreated. You may have decided that it isn't worth extending yourself. The problem with that is you become hard and crusty. You are the one losing in this scenario. Decide that no matter what, you will spread joy and remain open. You will give smiles, hold doors, and be as kind as you can. When you do this you feel good and that energy is contagious. You don't control anyone but yourself, and you choose to give. You raise everyone's energy when you keep your heart open and you give kindness. When you do this, the kindness that returns to you will be threefold.

MAKE it a habit

- Look for little ways to be kind on a regular basis.
- Practice smiling and saying good morning.
- Hold doors, and say thank you and hello more often.

37

Habit 34: Love People, Engage Them and Connect

"My humanity is bound up in yours, for we can only be human together."

—Bishop Desmond Tutu[1]

Don't just live your life—engage and participate in it full throttle. Look for the divine in all and let God take care of the rest. Connect with people's souls. When I attended a Diversity and Inclusion class with Franklin Covey, I learned about a tribe in Africa that greets each other with the phrase *Sawa Bona*, which means "I see you." Isn't that what we all want? To be seen? Isn't that why Facebook is so addicting? It is a place for us to be seen. The response to *Sawa Bona* is *Sikhona*, "I am here." The ancient belief is that until you see me, I don't exist.

I want you to think of a time when you felt invisible. Maybe you were standing at a store counter waiting to be served. Three people were behind the counter, but no one acknowledged you were standing there. You stayed calm for a bit, and then you began to get frustrated. "Don't they *see* me?" you say to yourself. "What, are they blind?" All you need is for one person to make eye contact with you for a split second, to hold up a hand to indicate, one moment please. All you need is to be seen and acknowledged.

People are fascinating. Everyone has a story, and everyone wants to be heard. People are hungry to connect. It is the reason people go to a bar or to a coffee shop alone. They could stay at home and drink coffee or have a cocktail, but they go out because they are want to connect with another human being.

Yet so many of us are so busy trying to look cool, be tough, or serious that we miss the chance to connect with each other. We sit on long airplane rides and never say hello to the person sitting next to us for three hours. We pass the same people in the hallways at our offices every day and we never make eye contact. I saw a news report the other day about a man who wanted to see how many interactions he could go through without ever saying a word to people. He went to the supermarket and bought a few items, they exchanged money and he left. Not a word was spoken. He went to the library and returned a book, and no one said a word. He realized that if he didn't want to he could go through almost an entire day interacting with people, but yet never speaking with them. "How sad!" I thought.

I suggest that you try to find something out about the people in your path. Not every day and everywhere, but by simply being open to connections, you will find opportunities to connect with people everywhere. The more open you are to meeting people, the bigger the chance you have of meeting someone who will have a positive influence on your life. It is said that each person knows approximately 300 people on a first-name basis. If you meet 20 new people in one week, you are in effect connecting to 6,000 people.

Use your best judgement and know when to back off, when to engage with someone, and when to let him or her speak. I once heard a speaker say, "The worst kind of death is to be talked to death." And Dale Carnegie wrote, "you can make more friends in two months by being interested in other people than you can in two years by trying to get other people interested in you."[2] So if this is a new habit for you, please take into account the response you get. If someone doesn't engage that easily, it is sometimes best to back off. To my surprise, people are often friendly, giving, and willing to tell you almost anything if you establish rapport.

I once heard Maya Angelou say on the Oprah Winfrey show that "Every single person on earth is saying . . .

. . . did you hear me?
. . . do you see me?
. . . do you really see me?
. . . does what I'm saying matter?
Every person matters."[3]

Every person matters! Ask yourself what does your face say to the people in your path. Life is a mirror, and if you aren't getting the reactions you want from people, the best thing you can do is ask yourself, what kind of energy, what facial expressions are you putting out? Whatever you are putting out in the world is exactly what you are getting in return.

We live in this web of interconnectedness, and if we are aware of this, we cherish each other and see each person as important. You can meet fabulous people everywhere you go just by being open to it. Most of these people you may never see again, but for the moment you will share your journey. I am constantly reminded that life is made up of moments and lived in the now.

Making connections with people is something that fills me deep in my soul. I enjoy connecting, bonding, and really getting to hear about a person's hopes, dreams, and fears. This can only happen by being willing to connect. Research has shown that the difference between moderately happy people and truly happy people is linked to strong relationships and connections. You make a connection with someone when a friend tells you he or she are there for you, or a coworker helps you with a task. Making connections is not only linked to happiness, but to better health and longer life.[4]

How can you incorporate this in your life? Make a commitment the next time you are in public to practice making eye contact. Once that feels comfortable, and it may take a while, say hello. No one will scold you for saying hello. Not everyone will say hello back, but who cares? You have to be okay with that. It is not the end of the world, and you will be surprised at how many people will say hello. Become aware of your posture, is it open or closed? If you walk around never making eye contact, looking at the ground with your arms crossed, and then wonder why you never meet anyone, you may want to look in the mirror. Work on having an open and inviting posture and have fun trying to meet new people.

Better yet, join a club, enroll in a class, or simply reach out to someone you see every day, but you never connected with. Invite them for coffee. In the documentary *Happy*, written, directed, and coproduced by Roko Belic, P. Read Montague, PhD, and professor of neuroscience at Baylor College of Medicine, talks about how when we connect and cooperate with each other, dopamine is released in our body. This naturally formed chemical he claims is measurable and gives our bodies the same reaction as a drug such as cocaine or the high that a sugary drink would gives us, yet it has no negative side affects. Social bonding and interaction, he says, are programmed to be intrinsically rewarding to humans.

When I watched the documentary and the Okinawan women spoke of how they connect, play, and support each other on a regular basis,[5]

I was moved to tears of joy. I could feel their happiness and their deep connection with each other. It was a palpable feeling as I witnessed their joy and connection. What they did for each other was simple, but powerful. They were there for each other. They met on a regular basis, they were involved in each other's lives, and when someone was down or going through a hard time, they all pitched in and helped the person out either by offering their time, listening, or helping them laugh again. The idea is for you to experience this on a regular basis yourself, and for you to make the commitment to connect with others.

MAKE it a habit

- Practice making eye contact or smiling.
- Give yourself a goal of saying hello to three strangers one week.
- Be aware of your posture and body language.

38

Habit 35: Be Flexible to Become Strong

"Thus, flexibility, as displayed by water, is a sign of life.
Rigidity, its opposite, is an indicator of death."

—Anthony Lawlor[1]

Would you rather be happy or right?

The dictionary defines "strong" as "able to withstand great force or pressure; possessing skills and qualities that create a likelihood of success."[2] It is said in our culture that only the strong survive.

There is something to be said for strength and power, but to truly be strong, it pays to learn to be flexible. An oak tree is strong, but in a harsh storm, the oak tree can be ripped out by its roots, as can many other types of trees. In comparison, a palm tree isn't that hard and solid, yet in a storm, the palm tree bends, enabling it to remain intact in hurricane-force winds. It is the flexibility that gives the palm tree its strength. It may lay down during a storm, but when the clouds clear, it stands up tall again.

Ego plays a huge role in our lives and many of us can't stand the idea of being wrong or to have someone disagree with us. We hold on to our opinions as if they define who we are. In an effort to appear strong, we become hard, dominating, and controlling. When someone doesn't agree with us, we fight hard to change his or her mind. As humans we can take a great lesson from the palm tree. Are there times in your life that you could benefit from being flexible? If happiness and peace is your goal, what is this fight worth in the long run? What if I was to flex, to allow and to accept that we have different views on the same thing? Does allowing another's opinion diminish me in any way? It does not; it actually makes you stronger.

Look for opportunities to bend and to be flexible. A person who is flexible is open to all possibilities. Be open to times that you can choose to let someone else have his or her way. Be flexible and allow yourself to contemplate others' opinions. When you are open to listening and considering the opinions of others, you become the type of person that people want to engage with. Your flexibility is attractive and encourages people to connect with you. When you are harsh, rigid, and stuck in your ways, people will avoid connecting with you and tiptoe around you in conversations.

The Buddhist believes that all human suffering comes from attachment. You not only grow attached to your home, your cars, and your relationships, but you attach yourself to your ideas, opinions, and titles. Let yourself be in a state of unattachment and a state of not knowing. This may sound contradictory to my previous advice about connecting. This is another dichotomy of living successfully. When you allow yourself to connect with another person, but not be attached to thinking that they should think and act like you all the time, or that you need to control them, you allow space for you to love each other and enjoy each other's company. Let what is going on around you flow like water. Water doesn't fight, get hard, or angry; it follows the path of least resistance. It flows easily and effortlessly until it gets where it needs to be. By allowing yourself to be flexible, you take on the same power as water.

I am reminded of a poem:

Here lies the body of William Jay
He died defending his right of way
He was right, dead right, as he sped along
But he is just as dead as if he was wrong.[3]

In other words, pick your battles. The more flexible you are the stronger you will be. This is a dichotomy that many people don't get. So many people believe that in order to be strong that they have to be rigid, hard, and tough, when often just the opposite is true. When you aren't attached to your opinion, you make room for other people to have a different point of view and there is so much strength and spiritual maturity in that.

I have been told that I am too nice. I don't agree with that. I am flexible and I don't always have to get my way. If something is of utmost importance to me, I am strong enough to stand up for what I want, but I don't feel the need to always be the decision maker or to be in control. I'm happy to let someone else be the expert, have opinions that differ from my own, and let them control the situation.

MAKE it a habit

- When someone expresses an opinion different than your own, practice saying, "That is an interesting way of looking at that. I've never seen it that way before." Then just let it go.
- Ask yourself what the benefit of being flexible can bring to the situation.
- Open yourself up to new and better opportunities.

39

Habit 36: Take Responsibility for Your Energy

"I really needed people to take responsibility for the kind of energy they brought me."

—Jill Bolte Taylor[1]

Years ago while rollerblading around Rockland Lake, I would pass this one woman who just had a certain glow about her. She was a tiny little thing and much older than me, but whenever we passed and said good morning, I noticed a sparkle in her eye, and a melody in her voice. Her energy was so loving and alive. One morning I stopped to talk to her and she was a bundle of delightful energy and love. Her name was Kaya and she was so full of life, optimism, and hope. Oh, and did I mention she was in her eighties? Her energy was just so amazing that I fell in love with her soul before I even knew her. She was so passionate, so loving, and so vibrant that I felt myself being attracted to her like a magnet.

Life is about how you are currently molding your energy. You are a magnet. You are pure energy. Whether you realize it or not, you are taking energy in and putting energy out in the world every moment. You are an attractor and the creator of your experience. The energy you put out affects every experience you have.

More important, you are in control of the vibrations you send out, and when you get this, a huge shift happens. When you take responsibility for your life, your reactions, and for the energy you bring into each situation, your life changes. Think of yourself as a thermostat. A thermostat sets the temperature of a room. It is different than a thermometer, which takes the temperature of the room. Many people will walk into a situation and assume the temperature of the room. If you walk into a room full of complaining miserable people, you start complaining right along with them. If you want to be a leader and be in control of your life, you must set the tone and the energy level.

Your physical being emits an energy that you are either conscious or unconscious of. The more conscious you are of this, the more you can guide your energy. I want you to imagine what people say to themselves when they see you walking down the hallway toward them, see your name on an email in their inbox, or see your name come up on their caller ID. Are they saying to themselves, "Oh good, here comes [insert your name]," or are they saying, "Ugh, what does she or he want now?"

Look for ways to use your energy to make people feel good about themselves and in the long run, you will feel better too. Use your energy with the checker at the grocery store; be pleasant and say something nice. If the checker is grumpy and not smiling, leave him or her one of your smiles and a kind word. You are not in control of the energy of the people around you, but you do control your own energy. You have the power to raise the energy of everyone around you with your presence. All you need to do is own your power and stay centered in a space of positive energy. Whenever you shine light in a dark place, the energy shifts and light prevails.

Your feelings of passion, joy, and optimism are all signs that you are on the right track. How someone treats you makes no difference as long as you stay conscious of the energy you emit. The rude, mean, and selfish people are still out in the world, but that doesn't have to be who you become. You can choose to help to bring out the best in people based on the energy you put out. Whenever you find yourself frustrated or upset, take a step back and look in the mirror and ask yourself how you have been showing up in the world. Realize that life isn't about tomorrow, it is about right now, and how you are choosing to use your energy in this moment. You have a choice.

How do you do this? Manage your energy by paying attention to your thoughts and taking responsibility for them. Listen to your body and pay attention to its many signals. When you are feeling frustrated or any negative emotion, bring back awareness to the present moment. Take a deep breath and look around. Realize that in this moment, everything is fine. The world is not crashing in on you, and any fear or anxiety you feel is usually associated with a thought you are thinking. Know that you have control over your conscious thoughts, so choose an empowering thought to replace your thought of fear. This helps to reset your energy level and prevent you from ruminating.

Dogs are great teachers of this concept. A dog lives in the present moment. I remember how excited my dog Naui would be every day when I got home from work. His tail would start wagging the minute he heard my car in driveway. I couldn't see this, but I knew it. He would greet me at the front door with so much enthusiasm, you would think he hadn't seen me for years. Some mornings I would leave him, get to my car, and realize I forgot something in the house. When I would open the front door he would greet me as if I had been gone all day. "Doesn't he realize it's been less than a minute?"

Dogs live in the moment, and in this moment they are elated to see you, regardless of how much time passed. Dogs are pure, happy energy because they live in the now. They aren't ruminating about the past or worrying about the future. They are here now.

When your energy is high, you will feel loving, happy, and open to new experiences. You will feel passion for your life. Look for ways to feed your passion and keep your energy up. Consciously notice the things that bring you joy and then make it a point to keep them in your life on a regular basis. Tune in to your heart and follow your energy and it will lead you exactly where you need to go. Think of yourself as an artist, and your medium is the energy you emit. When you are able to connect with that place, you will find yourself in a state of pure bliss and creativity. You are an artist of being alive, full of love, light, and positive energy.

This goes not only for when you are interacting with people but for everything in your life. Make a conscious effort to bring positive empowering energy to all your endeavors. When you guide your energy to be positive, you will guide your experiences to be positive. The energy that you bring to a situation is exactly the energy that will become the situation. For example, if you drag yourself to an event telling yourself on the way over that this is something you are dreading and it is going to be awful, most likely you will experience exactly that. On the flip side if you are going to be at the event anyway, why not tell yourself that you are going to have a good time no matter what. If you do this, your energy will follow. You can use your energy to create positive experiences or negative experiences. In the end, the choice is yours. It always is.

As for Kaya and I, we have become good friends and she just recently celebrated her 90th birthday. Whenever I spend any time with Kaya I leave feeling happier and more aware of the beauty that surround me. She always talks of the magic of trees, the stars, the flowers, and the beauty of the earth. She leaves me singing voice mails when she calls. Even when she is down, she finds something to be grateful for. She is my energy role model.

MAKE it a habit

- Acknowledge that other people are reflecting back to you the energy that you are putting out, and if you don't like what you are receiving, it is up to you to change your energy.
- For one full day, focus on setting the tone wherever you go—be the thermostat.
- Work at leaving people feeling better for being in your space.

40

Habit 37: Nourish Your Passion

"Nothing great in the world has been accomplished without passion."

—Georg Wilhelm Friedrich Hegel[1]

The definition of "passion" is "a strong and barely controllable emotion."[2] Passion is everything. Without it you can't accomplish anything that speaks to your soul. You can check off a long list of accomplishments but you will never be satisfied. When you mix passion with effectiveness you then have a winning combination. I have a hard time articulating what passion is, but I know it when I feel it. I'm not talking about romantic passion, but the passion you experience when an idea hits you, when you have an aha moment, or when your heart feels so filled up with love and joy you just have to let it out. That is passion. Passion motivates and excites you to reach, to do, and to go beyond what you thought possible. Passion gives you the energy and the belief in yourself to listen to your heart and follow its advice. I may not be able to give you passion, but I can point you in the right direction.

How do you nurture your passion? There are so many ways. Read. Write. Listen to music. Watch movies that inspire you. Engage in deep and meaningful conversations. Travel. Open yourself up to unlimited possibilities. If you are waiting for someone to ignite your passion, what happens if they never show up? Do you have a muse? If not, be one for yourself. Work to ignite your passions regularly and feed them every day. Pick up a book and let a passage inspire you and give you hope or direction. Books inspire you when they speak to your soul, your passion, your purpose, or your heart. The simple words on a page can reignite the flame that burns in your soul. Books can help you identify those burning desires of your heart that you find difficult to articulate. You read the words on the page, and suddenly you feel your heart beat faster and your skin dances with the realization that someone has put your feelings into words. When you find your passion dwindling, get another book. It is up to you to keep your passion alive and to find ways to feed it. If books aren't your thing, feed your passion with movies that have an uplifting message, one that feed you and ignites your own passions and dreams.

Purposely seek out positive, uplifting music. Music touches you on such a deep and profound level. It gets to the core of who you are and engages all your senses. Use it as a tool to ignite your passion.

Write, write, write.

Capture your ideas, your dreams, and the deep feelings in your heart. I have an entire section on journaling. Writing keeps your passion alive. When you write you connect your mind and your body with your dreams and your passion is fed. You can write down whatever you wish. Your journal or writing tablet is your very own scared space where you can let your imagination run wild. Writing is a life force all on its own and when you are writing about something you are passionate about, you come alive.

The word "enthusiasm" comes from the Greek word *entheo*, which comes from two Greek words: *en*, meaning "inside," and *theos*, meaning "God."[3] This translates into the God inside. When you are passionate and enthusiastic you are being lifted to a higher space. You are exhibiting the spirit of God within yourself. When you feel this excitement and passion grow within you, I believe that this is God's way of telling you that you are on the right path.

There are so many ways to connect with your passion, but each of us must find our own path. A friend of mine loves to play the mandolin and fence while another friend I know competes in triathlons and Ironman competitions. Painting, quilting, golfing, teaching, fishing, volunteering, the list can go on and on. What feeds your passion is a personal experience, but one that you will recognize once you are conscious of it. Often I hear from people who tell me that they have lost touch with their passions. They have let the needs of their family, work, and everyday life get in the way. I understand how true this can be, but I challenge you to make time for your passions.

A woman admitted in my class recently that she had not worked out in over a year and was using her children and family as an excuse. When she sat in my class it suddenly dawned on her that her husband still made the time to work out, and that if he could make the time so could she. No one was stopping her but herself. Are you stopping yourself from doing what you love and feeding your passion? Have you disconnected with your passions over the years? Do you not know what they are? Start now by asking yourself and paying attention to the activities and things that light you up.

Talk to people who share your passion. Don't waste time trying to convince people about what you are passionate about. If they don't agree, it isn't worth your energy. Instead seek out people who already believe and are excited to talk with you about your passion and your ideas. The right people are everywhere when you are open to finding them. Feed your passion regularly, just like you feed your body.

"Throw your heart over the fence and the rest will follow."

—Norman Vincent Peale[4]

MAKE it a habit

- Feed your passion every day by taking time for the things you love.
- Trust that your passion is God or the universe speaking to you.
- Create rituals around the activities you are passionate about.

41

Habit 38: Say Yes to Adventure and Leave Your Comfort Zone

"I arise in the morning torn between the desire to improve the world and a desire to enjoy the world. This makes it hard to plan the day."

—E. B. White[1]

There is a great, big world out there and so many people limit themselves to their own backyard. The more I travel, the more I realize just how much of the world I haven't experienced. I learn so much on each trip about the places and the people I visit, and about myself. I love to travel, but I don't necessarily like to travel by myself, because it takes me out of my comfort zone. Yet, I often have to get places by myself. I still feel the fear of the unknown, or the awkwardness of being a stranger in a strange place, but I tell myself to get over it and move forward. I had to learn to leave my comfort zone in order to experience something new and have a new adventure.

I work at leaving my comfort zone and pushing myself to have new adventures. I have gone to the movies by myself, traveled to Spain alone, and even went to Greece for two weeks with a person I barely knew. I push myself to talk to people I don't know, try new foods, and try new sports. Yes, I have had a little trepidation at first, but I force myself to live and to not be afraid. As a result, the memories I have amassed are priceless.

I remember one night I was on the rooftop in Seville, Spain, hanging my laundry on the clothesline and I was filled with such a sense of joy and magic. I laughed to myself wondering what was it that made hanging laundry on the line so much special in Spain? Another time I sat on the front steps of my room in Mykonos, Greece. As I looked down the white-washed streets in the night, a baby cried loudly from the apartment upstairs, a woman beat the dust off her carpet on another balcony, and I felt my heart leap and my skin dance. It was a magical place, and I fell in love with it. Maybe the thrill was just the experience of something new, of being able to leave my comfort zone. Getting out of your comfort zone forces you to tune into your senses, and this gives you a greater sense of being alive. When you are in your routine and always doing the same thing, life may feel dull or boring. So while I am encouraging you to create positive habits, some that you will repeat every day, I am also encouraging you to make seeking adventure a habit as well.

In order to have these experiences, you have to learn how to leave your comfort zone, and I guarantee you that what you will gain from leaving that zone will be priceless.

My first day in a new country is often a bit overwhelming, but after 24 hours I acclimate and enjoy the experience. My first day in Cuernavaca, Mexico, was one of those times. I was alone and unfamiliar with the neighborhood. I didn't know if it was safe or not, but I chose to go for a walk to get a handle on where I was. I kept looking over my shoulder and kept my guard up as I walked down the street. It was a loud place, and many of the cars that passed me were honking their horns and yelling in Spanish out their windows at me. It was a hot summer day in July, and I soon learned that women in this city don't wear shorts. I was wearing shorts, which provoked all the yelling. It took me a day or so to get comfortable with my surroundings, and once I did, I enjoyed the magic and the gift of the experience. Once I got my bearings, the rest of the trip was fabulous.

Adventure can mean different things to different people, but the point is to say YES to life, and say yes to trying something different. Are you stuck in a rut? Do you do the same things all the time? Do you eat at the same restaurants, spend time with the same people, and drive the same roads day in and day out? The only thing you are going to find in a rut is other rut dwellers. You don't have to leave the country to get out of your comfort zone, but you do have to leave your backyard. It can be as simple as trying a different restaurant, or maybe just ordering something different at your usual restaurant. I have a good friend who orders chicken parmigiana everywhere we go. How limiting is that? It doesn't take away from the quality of his life, and if that is all he ever does, he'll be fine. But imagine what could happen if he tries something new?

We all have a comfort zone. This is where you feel most at home and comfortable. Unfortunately, the only difference between a comfort zone and a grave are the dimensions. Ouch! Your comfort zone is the place in your life that requires no effort on your part. It is easy. You get up, go to the same job, eat lunch with the same people, go home to the same house and watch the same shows on television at night. The next day you repeat the same drill and so goes the days of your life. Big ouch!

In order to get out of your comfort zone, you have to invest some effort, and that can be hard for some people. You can start small or take a big leap. Take a new route to work, start a conversation up with a stranger, or try a new sport or activity. This doesn't sound so hard, yet so many don't do it. Why then are we so hung up on staying in the same place? Like I said earlier, to leave our comfort zone takes effort, and often effort is uncomfortable. To start up a conversation with a stranger puts you at the risk of them not responding nicely to you. To try a new sport makes you an amateur, and might I add, a fool. There I said it. That is what we are all so afraid of: looking like a fool. To learn anything new, you must first be the novice. You have to start somewhere.

Let yourself be the fool. Let go of your worries about what other people think of you. If you think about the people in your life that you admire, I would bet you that they have big personalities, that they are bold, and they take risks. You watch them from afar, secretly wanting to be them, but never making a move. If you look closely at their lives, you will see that they have probably played the fool more then once, made a mistake, and blurted out something inappropriate and in the end survived. So let go of your fears of looking foolish. People who live their lives fully make lots of mistakes.

The exciting part about leaving your comfort zone is the high that comes with accomplishing something new. The first time I went scuba diving I felt like a superhero, and I could accomplish anything. Now this was after feeling foolish and very scared. I can vividly remember the first time I put my regulator in my mouth. I was in Antigua in the West Indies and I had just taken what we call in the scuba diving world, a quick "resort course." This is a short course that gives you as little information as possible to enable you to go scuba diving within a few hours without having to take the six-month certification course. I recall the instructor telling us not to ascend too fast because our lungs might explode and to not do something else for fear of that our eyes may pop out. He said it in a cheerful, kidding manner to make light of the situation, but I knew he was serious. Needless to say, I was scared, but I was trying desperately not to show it. I was taken out on boat into the beautiful blue waters, but I really didn't notice the beauty around me because I was worried and scared. I was sick to my stomach, but I was determined to move out of my comfort zone. I got into the water and was instructed to go below the surface. I took a few huge extra gulps of air as if doing so would give me some reserves of air. This of course was an illusion. I put the regulator in my mouth and went down. My heart was pounding so fast, and I told myself to just breathe. Breathe in. Breathe out. Breathe in. Breathe out. It was then I noticed that nothing bad was happening to me. Air was flowing through my lungs just as if I was on land. This helped me to calm down and start to enjoy the experience. I had moved through my fear and left my comfort zone. Yahooo! When I got back on that boat, I felt like a rock star and I now had a new and improved expanded comfort zone. I later went on to take an official scuba course to get certified, and it has afforded me some of the best and most unique experiences of my life.

When you face the unknown and succeed, your confidence grows. That is the true gift to be gained from leaving your comfort zone. This confidence affects every other area of your life. Once you learn a new skill, try a new sport, or open yourself up to trying something new, you ask yourself, "If I can do this, what else can I do?" This is a glorious feeling and where true growth takes place. This new place becomes your new comfort zone.

So where are you holding yourself back? What adventure or new experience have you always wanted to try? What is your dream and what are you waiting for? Don't wait. You will notice that once you actually put your toe in the water, as I did in my scuba diving example, the fear will go away.

MAKE it a habit

- Every day for one week, do something you have never done before.
- Take notice that when you do something foolish, you survive and life goes on.
- Expect the best.

42

Habit 39: Make Time for Recovery and Refueling

"When you die, your inbox will be full."

—Unknown wise person

My first job out of college was for an advertising agency. It was an extremely busy office, and so often, just as I was about to leave for the day, an emergency project would land on my desk. The work never ended, and so in my infinite wisdom I thought that if I skipped my lunch, I would be able to finish my work on time and go home. This went on for months. After a while I stopped taking my breaks too. I was miserable and still not able to leave on time. One day I decided to go to the park on my lunch break and eat outside. I couldn't believe how much better I felt when I got back to the office. That hour break was exactly what I needed to have a clear mind and be more productive in the afternoon. You are kidding yourself if you think you too don't need to take a break.

How are you doing right now? Are you still with me? Are you tired? Do you need a break? Well, if you have made it this far, you deserve a break. And I'm going to tell you that you deserve a break every day and often. What? Every day? Yes, that is right, every day. We have become far too accustomed to a binge and purge way of life. We put in too many hours for months and then think all the damage and stress that we put on our bodies can be remedied with a weekend at the spa. Unfortunately, it isn't that easy.

We are Americans after all, and our country was founded on our work ethic. We work hard, we work long hours, and if we still aren't happy with what we have, we work some more. We brag about how busy we are, how we never have time for ourselves, and the fact that we are carrying our vacation days over. We over-schedule ourselves and worse than that, we over-schedule our children. We are even hard on each other. When a coworker has the guts to leave the office at 5:00, we chuckle, look at our watch, and say, "What, half a day for you?"

Your body needs time to recover, and guess what, so does your mind. You need to schedule little breaks in your day. The simple act of standing up every hour increases your metabolism and gets your blood flowing.

I had a teacher who told me the plum and the straw theory. She said that when we wake up in the morning each of us is like a big juicy plum and that everyone that comes toward us during the day has a straw in their mouth. Each person sucks a little bit of life out of us, until at the end of the day what remains is this dried-up prune. "What are you going to do to plump back up?" she asked.

This is why recovery breaks are necessary throughout your day. If I asked you to think back over the last 48 hours, think about how much of yourself you have given to others. You have given time to your family and your career. You have given your advice, your ear, your support, your ideas, your muscle, and a whole host of other things. Like anything else when you are giving, giving, giving, at some point you have to put some of that energy back.

My first suggestion is that you take a proper lunch break. It has become normal for people to eat lunch at their desk or to not take a lunch at all. You tell yourself you are being efficient, but you are doing yourself a huge disservice when you don't take a lunch break. Even if you don't work, taking a break for lunch is still important.

Taking a lunch break not only feeds your body, but it feeds your mind and refocuses you for the rest of your day. In addition to your lunch break, I want you to take many breaks during the day. Get up from your desk, get away from your work area, stretch, walk, and simply clear your mind. You will find that you will be much more productive if you do. Your body was built to move, not to sit and stagnate all day.

Take a real vacation, and by this I mean one where you aren't constantly tied to the office the whole time checking and responding to emails. Take the time to reflect on your life. By this I mean taking some time out of your week, your month, your year to ask yourself, "What is working? What needs improvement? How are you doing?" These are critical questions, and yet 95 percent of people never ask them. They just keep doing the same thing year after year, and wonder why they can't get ahead. Taking time out to reflect is something I started years ago, along with goal setting, and it is a fabulous teacher. You can't afford not to reflect.

Learn the art of making your own hours. The one thing I learned many years ago is that everything is negotiable. If you are a good worker and you work for a fair boss, and you deliver results, they will often give you more space than you realize to create your own schedule. You must first become an invaluable resource. You do this by completing everything you need precisely and on time.

Did you ever notice that when you have a vacation planned, you are extremely efficient and effective the week before you leave? You make sure all your "i's" are dotted and your "t's" are crossed because you want to enjoy your time off. My question to you is why then don't you work like that every week? So much time is wasted because we aren't focused on what needs to be accomplished. When you are organized, focused, and take steps toward your goals, you are met with success. There is a saying that the amount of time allowed for a task is the amount of time it will take to complete. Meaning if you have seven hours that is how long task abc will take, but if you only have three hours, you will still be able to complete it.

You will find that your best ideas come to you when you are relaxed and centered. Most people tell me they get the best ideas in the shower, while out on a walk, or when they first wake up. It is impossible to get to that centered place if you are always running, doing, and going. Organizations expect people to think outside the box and be creative, and yet they never give them any time to disconnect during the day.

Make it a habit to create space in your day, take breaks, and recover. You will come back to work more focused, centered, and alert.

MAKE it a habit

- Take your lunch break as many times a week as possible.
- Every hour get up from your desk, or leave your work area and walk around and take a mental break.
- Don't respond to emails while on vacation unless absolutely necessary.

43

Habit 40: Drink Water

"Water is the driving force of all nature."

—Leonardo da Vinci[1]

Here is another habit you must have heard a million times. It has been recommended that you drink eight 8-ounce glasses of water a day for good health. So I ask you, do you do it? If so, that is great. If not. Why not? Drinking water increases your energy, it improves your metabolism, detoxifies your organs, and much more.[2] Do I need to go on? Pay attention to your body. Take notice of how you feel when you drink water, versus how you feel when you don't. You will find that your muscles aren't as achy, your stomach seems to digest better, and your skin and hair look better.

How to make sure you get enough water is simple. Learn the measurement of every glass in your cabinet. Pay attention to what glass or container appeals to you and aids you in drinking more water. I have found that I will drink more from a water bottle with a straw than I will from a glass. I purchased myself a bottle that I love and that I carry around with me everywhere. I keep track in my head, and quite honestly it is not that hard. If you lose count, don't stress, simply look at your urine. When it is clear or very light, you know that you are drinking enough water. When it is dark, or yellow/orange in color, you know that you have not.

I can hear you moaning right now that when you drink too much water you have to go to the bathroom too often. Is that true? Yes and no. It is true that you will need a few more bathroom breaks in the beginning, but over time your body will adjust and you will be fine. So throw that excuse out the window and get over it. The fact that you are relieving yourself more is a good thing because that means your body is flushing your system out. This will aid you in weight loss if that is your goal and help you fight against colds and flu. If you add a little lemon to your water, it will aid in your digestion. The better hydrated you are, the more lubricated your joints and muscles will be and you will be less likely to cramp.

MAKE it a habit

- Keep a glass of water on your night stand and drink it first thing upon waking up in the morning.
- Buy yourself a nice glass or water bottle.
- Keep track and monitor your urine color.

44

Habit 41: Know How to Find Your Center

"At the center of your being you have the answer; you know who you are and you know what you want."

—Lao Tzu[1]

Being peaceful and centered does not mean that everything in your life is going perfectly and that you have no obstacles. Being centered is when, in midst of a storm, you can find a peaceful space. When you don't let yourself get emotionally hijacked, and when you are able to back up from a situation to see it clearly enough to know that no matter what happens you will be okay and that you can accept this moment exactly as it is. The situation is secondary. You can let your emotions run you and flit about like a crazy fool, or you can stand strong in your core, find your center, and weather the storm gracefully. This comes from being conscious to what is happening, versus responding unconsciously. This comes from being present in your own life and creating space between what is happening and what you are thinking and feeling.

What it comes down to is acceptance. When you accept whatever life has handed you and you remain centered and conscious, you are in a better position to deal with your circumstances. For example, if you are driving down the road at 65 mph and you get a flat tire, you can curse, scream, engage your fight and flight, and run your blood pressure up. Or you can accept that this is happening to you in this present moment. Once you have accepted the circumstances, you can access your center, find the strength to deal with the situation, and take the appropriate steps. Acceptance of the situations makes your actions intelligent and not reactive. When you fight what is, you are just setting yourself up for frustration and stress. You always have a choice to center and empower yourself in every situation. The wise person learns to relax in the unknown.

You have been given your flight and fight responses for a reason and back in the early days of man. Your fight and flight reflexes were usually turned on when something was a life or death situation. You might be in danger from a wild animal and your senses would tell you to run and flee the scene. Adrenaline would then be released from your nervous system and send all your energy to your limbs, your arms and legs, so that you could get out of danger's way quickly. In modern society you don't experience those same life or death scenarios nearly as often, but yet as a society we are more stressed out than ever. Our fight and flight response is turned on daily when we are stuck in traffic, when we are running late for an appointment, or when we get bad news. Even though it is not a real life and death situation, your body responds as if it is and turns on your fight and flight response. Every time your fight and flight engages, in your body's attempt to save you, your stress hormones actually turn off your immune system to allow all your blood and energy to go to your arms and legs. In addition, when you are stressed, you begin to operate using reflexive behavior and because of this you are actually less intelligent.[2]

One way to find your center is to bring your awareness back to your breath. Inhaling through your nose for a count of eight and then exhaling through your mouth slows down your pulse in most cases and starts to calm you down.

Taking a deep breath forces you to back up from what you are feeling and thinking and create some space to choose. Stop what you are doing and pay attention to the voice in your head. Most likely it isn't feeding you empowering thoughts, and as you know by now, you have a choice of what you think. Choose a thought that calms you and tells you that you are fine. Create an affirmation and repeat it to yourself over and over again.

Close your eyes and visualize yourself in a scene from your past when you were totally calm and at peace. Where are you? For me the ocean always calms me down, and when I am off center, I visualize myself floating in the ocean. Almost immediately I can feel myself calm down. Where is your peaceful place? Is it the ocean, maybe high on a mountain top, in a field, or in your own backyard? Visualize it in your mind in full detail and use all of your senses to help take your mind there and your body will follow. I use this technique when I am sitting in traffic, in the dentist chair, and when I find myself upset over this or that. I talk to my wise self and say that getting upset will not help anything, and that if I can be calm in the midst of what is happening, I will experience a better outcome. This habit overlaps some of the others, for example, E+R=O or Guide Your Thoughts. So if your are already practicing them, this is a simple addition and a different way of looking at yourself.

MAKE it a habit

- Stop and take three to five deep breaths.
- Create an empowering affirmation.
- Visualize yourself in a calm place.

45

Habit 42: Use Your Words Wisely

"If someone were to pay you ten cents for every kind word you ever spoke and collect from you five cents for every unkind word, would you be rich or poor?"

—Unknown wise person[1]

Your words are powerful. They can be used as a tool build someone up or tear them down. We often throw around the English language haphazardly, and when we hurt someone we say, "they were *only* words." Most of us learned the saying, "sticks and stones can break my bones, but words can never hurt me." Unfortunately we have also learned how false that is. Words do hurt. I choose to use my words to build people up. I think back to the words that meant so much to me growing up.

My grandmother always told me how beautiful I was and how good I looked in every outfit I ever wore. Every greeting card she sent me was filled with her handwriting at the bottom telling me that I was smart, beautiful, and the joy of her life. My mother would write me notes about how much she loved me on the napkin that she put in my lunch bag for school each day. I was so blessed to have the influence these two wonderful women's words. At the time I never realized how powerful they were.

Words are free but have so much value. If you want to MAKE it a great day, make sure you look to make someone else's day, because whatever you put out in the world is exactly what is returned to you. Tell the people closest to you that you love them. Tell the woman next to you on the train that you adore her shoes. Tell the mailman you appreciate his hard work. Never stop using your words to build people up.

When a friend is going through a hard time, tell them you believe in them. Tell them that this too shall pass. You don't have to solve their problems. You just have to give them some hope. When someone is having a hard time they start to doubt themselves and their magnificence. A good friend is someone who reminds them of all their gifts and talents when they have lost their way. It is amazing how what you say to someone can turn their mood around, their day around, and even their life around.

The reason I am in this career is because of the words my mentor spoke to me. She always told me that I had talent and that I could use my talent to help inspire and educate others. Her words encouraged me to go back to school, to start my own business, and to believe in myself. I can say that, without a doubt, if she didn't use her words to encourage me I would still be working a nine-to-five job and not using my talents and strengths to serve others. But she saw something in me and she encouraged me to follow my dreams. I did all the work, but her words fueled my journey. That is the energy of words. Over the years there have been times that she has said things to me that I didn't want to hear because they stung, but even then, they were words I needed to hear to get better and keep growing.

Sometimes when people are behaving rudely or not treating me or someone else with respect, I want to use my words to hurt them and to take them down a notch. I have to remind myself that it is not my job to fix everyone and to teach them a lesson. I know within my heart that I have been put here to help people, to lift them up, and to make them see how beautiful they are. When people are rude to others, or to me for that matter, I instead try to find compassion. I tell myself that I really don't know what they are going through, what their struggles are, and why they feel the need to tear someone else down. I can tell you that when people feel bad about themselves, that is usually when they seek to hurt other people. I don't condone their behavior, but I can understand where it stems from if I look at them with a compassionate heart.

I know that for the most part everyone is simply doing the best they can. They might not be behaving the way I'd like, but I know they are doing their best. You usually don't wake up in the morning and say, "Hey, I'd really like to screw up someone's day today." But despite our best efforts, we do screw up other people's days. We do make mistakes. We use words that hurt and disappoint each other. I try to remind myself that each and every person is out here trying to make something of themselves and trying to bring meaning to their life. Every person has a dream and we are all doing the best we can.

When you are having a bad day and there is no one around to give you encouragement, use your words on yourself. Stop letting your "self" talk to you and start talking to your "self." Your inner critic is often being negative and not supporting you, but your words have power. Use them for your own good. Talk to your brain just like you would a child. Tell your brain that you know it thinks this is a good use of your time, but that you don't want to give this thought anymore energy. Ask your brain for a more empowering thought. You have to talk to yourself and ask for what you want. Use your affirmations.

When you are struggling to figure out a problem, use your words to ask your brain for help. Say something like, "Brain, you've always helped me in the past and I'm having some trouble figuring this out. Can you give me some new ideas on how I should [fill in the blank]?" Your brain is a marvelous tool when you use it to your advantage. So talk to it, talk to your wise self, the self inside you that knows all your deepest desires. Ask for help, ask for guidance, and tell yourself what you want and need to hear.

Tell yourself how fabulous you are, how smart you are, and how you are striving to be a better person. I talk to myself all day long, as most of us do, but I consciously tell myself things I want to hear, things that build me up and motivate me to go another step, walk another mile, and give more than is expected of me.

Thank your brain for all the good ideas and advice it has given you and encourage it to continue on that path. You can start to separate yourself from your thoughts and realize that just because a thought entered your brain doesn't mean you have to accept it. You always have choice, which is what this whole book is about. One of the most powerful sayings I've heard is that whatever you do to someone else, you also do to yourself. In other words, what you put out is what you get back. Once words are spoken, they can't be taken back, so use them wisely.

MAKE it a habit

- For one day look for opportunities to use your words to build someone up.
- Once a month send a card or note to someone with words of encouragement, love, and hope.
- For one day step back and look at the people in your life. Identify their true gifts and talents and then tell them out loud.

46

Habit 43: Make Time to Play

"We are always getting ready to live, but never living."

—Ralph Waldo Emerson[1]

When was the last time you swung on a swing, rode a bike, or licked an ice cream cone? Do you make time to play? You know the old saying, "all work and no play makes Jack a dull boy"? In today's world of technology it is so easy to busy yourself and not even know where the time has gone. We are constantly on Facebook, texting, on the Internet, or plugged in to some type of technology. Over the years I have made a commitment to play, to go outside, and to walk barefoot on the grass. I want to see and feel as much of the world as I can every day. All the things I did as a child are still fun today. I still have sleepovers with my girlfriends. We drink wine instead of soda, but the giggles are still the same.

On my 47th birthday I threw myself a party and asked everyone to bring a gift for a four- or a seven-year-old (47) that I would donate to a charity. I told them to be prepared to play like children. I went to the party store and bought princess napkins and pink paper plates, balloons, and streamers. I decorated my home like I would have if I was throwing a party for a seven-year-old. I wanted to play pin the tail on the donkey, but when I went to the party store, I couldn't find one, so I settled for pin the sunglasses on the Barbie. I bought a Mr. Potato Head and wrapped him up with layers of wrapping paper so that we could play hot potato, and I got a princess pinata that I filled with candy and some adult goodies. I wish you could have seen what a bunch of adults look like playing pin the sunglasses on the Barbie. It was so much fun, and I realized how impossible that game actually is. How anyone does it without cheating is beyond me. We all had honest to goodness belly laughs.

You don't have to play kids games if that isn't your thing. There are plenty of things you can do that are fun for adults. The problem is so many adults have forgotten how to play and have a good time. I can take that one step further to say that many people don't know how to have a good time anymore if alcohol isn't involved. So many activities are centered around drinking, and while I love a glass of wine, I drink to be social and not to get drunk, and not even to get buzzed. I don't need alcohol to have a good time. If you start to think about the last few times you had fun and you realize that you had had a little too much to drink, you might want to slow down or seek help if needed. I want you to think about what activities bring you joy, fun, and are playful. Do you know what they are?

Make a list of the top ten things that bring you joy.

1._____
2._____
3._____
4._____
5._____
6._____
7._____
8._____
9._____
10._____

One of the traits of happy people is that they take time to play and to savor life's joys. The definition of the word "savor" is to enjoy something completely.[2] This happens when you are present in the moment and all your senses are focused on what you are doing. You can buy a really nice piece of chocolate, but if you eat it walking down the hall to a meeting while talking on your cell phone, you just missed the entire experience. To be present and to savor something means you are tuned in to what you are doing. Children do this when they play. They aren't worrying about what is going to happen after dinner; they are in the moment and blissful. Playing and savoring life's experiences can do the same for you. It takes effort to tune in and pay attention. It takes a conscious decision to slow down and take in a sunset, a sip of your morning coffee, or sound of a bird. When you do, you can relish an ordinary experience such as eating a nice meal.

Have you forgotten how to play? Ask yourself what was fun for you before the Internet, video games, and Facebook were invented? How did you play as a child when your mom made you go outside? What did people do before television and radio were invented? Hmmmm, gives you something to think about, doesn't it? I know for me as a child, my brother, sister, and I would lay on the ground and make pictures out of the clouds; we would play tag games and make go-carts out of old baby carriages. My sister makes it a point to play with her kids all the time. She doesn't just sit back and watch them play, she joins in and gets involved. She gets right down on floor with them, goes down the slide, and has her face painted too. Play is how you define it. Savoring is what keeps you present. To this day I still love to do a cartwheel on a freshly mowed lawn, lay on my back under a tree, and look up at the beautiful patterns that the leaves form. I play cards with my friends, color with my niece, and my all-time favorite, drawing pictures with colored chalk on the driveway. You can savor any moment you choose. Research has shown that people who savored ordinary experiences were more confident, extroverted, and overall happier.

Get out of your head for a little while and let yourself play like a child.

MAKE it a habit

- Make a list of the top ten things that bring you joy.
- Schedule play dates with yourself and friends. Find fun things to do.
- Revisit your childhood games and activities to see if any would be fun for you today.

47

Habit 44: Create Relationship Rituals

*"As long as you remember the person who loved you, and
whom you still love, then you're making love endure."*

—Guillaume Musso[1]

If you've read this far, I'm hoping you have begun to start creating positive habits for yourself. In this final habit, I would like you to think about the habits you have in your relationship. So often couples fall into ruts, grow apart, and wake up one day and wonder where the magic of their relationship went. I can speak from experience, because it happened to me. When Steve and I first fell in love, it was pure magic. We complimented each other in so many ways, and our sense of adventure kept us discovering, traveling, growing, and loving. I would have sworn to you that our love was a love of a lifetime and that we would be together forever. As you know, we didn't have a happy ending. We got settled into a routine, life got in the way, and we created bad habits around our relationship. Habits that kept us busy working, going, and doing, but separate and not connecting. I think many couples can relate to this. Once you get home from work after a long day, you are tired. If you have children, your work has just begun. You make dinner, help with homework, do some laundry, get the kids off to bed, and then collapse in front of the television, too tired to even talk. You aren't connecting, bonding, or being present with each other. This is where good couple habits can help you.

The first relationship habit that I suggest is that you set some guidelines about how to disagree and how to have an argument. If you are in a relationship long enough, you will have disagreements. Get into the habit of never using certain phrases or words that cut deep. You don't want to say something you will regret later. I did this with my former husband one night in the heat of my anger. I can't recall exactly what I said, but it was something to the effect of not caring whether he left for good or not. Remember what I just said about using your words wisely? I didn't do a good job here. I didn't mean it literally, but I said it and I couldn't take it back. Years later when we were in couples counseling and trying to get ourselves back on track, those words came back to haunt me. It was in that moment that I realized that I should have never said them. At the time I was angry and hurt and I wanted him to hurt too, so I said something that I knew would sting. I have since learned how wrong I was.

In my new relationship with Gary, I have promised myself to never utter words or phrases filled with hate or disgust aimed toward him. No matter what I am angry about, I remind myself that I love Gary with all my heart and that after my anger dissipates, the love will still be there. I am a work in progress, and I can still have a temper from time to time. Only now when I get frustrated, angry, or upset, I create space between myself and my anger and I use the E+R=O technique I wrote about. If I have nothing nice to say, I work at saying nothing and staying silent until I can create some space around what has happened. I ask myself what I want. Do I want to be right, or do I want to be happy? In the end, I want to be happy. I want to be in love and I want to share my life with Gary. This is the outcome I want, so I then have to choose a response that will keep me and us on that track.

A habit that Gary has instituted, and I absolutely love, is to go to bed a half hour before we want to go to sleep. We use this time to reconnect, cuddle, and spend some time with each other. Often when we get home from work, there is still so much to do. We are together in the same house, but we aren't present with each other. I'm running one way and he is running the other. This time before we go to sleep allows us to be present and in the moment. Sometimes words are spoken, but other times it feels so wonderful just to be held quietly. The part about this that I want you to understand is that we make the time for this.

I suggest that you and your partner create a ritual together where you can carve out some time and give each other your full attention. It may only be once a week if you have a large family and a demanding job, but it is so critical to keep this bond alive. Set a night aside, an hour or whatever you can to be with your partner to listen to them and really hear how they are, what their day was like, and what's on their mind. Use Habit 35: Love People, Engage Them and Connect. Be there and listen deeply. When someone listens to us wholeheartedly we feel seen, valued, and understood. The best gift you can give another person is the gift of your attention.

We are also in the habit of creating what we call "love names." They are the same as nicknames, but we use them to express our love to each other. Some are silly, some are wonderfully romantic, and others are downright sexy. I just love when Gary uses one of the "love names" he has created for me. It makes me feel special and cherished. I feel so worthy of his love and adoration. I can tell he loves it too, so I make a point of using the "love names" I've invented for him when I text him, call him on the phone, and any time I think of it. When I call Gary by one of his "love names" it brings such a smile to his face, and it makes me happy inside.

You can create many rituals together, and you can be as creative as you wish. These are just a few of ours. The importance of theses rituals to your relationship is that they keep you connected, bonded, and feeling valued. You have chosen this person as the one special person in your life. Make sure you don't let the other demands of your life crowd them out.

MAKE it a habit

- Set guidelines around how you will disagree.
- Agree that you won't use hateful language when you disagree.
- Create a ritual for connecting and being present.
- Select special "love names" for each other and use them often.

Conclusion

If you made it this far I applaud you. You have made an investment in yourself and your life. If I have done my job, you are ahead of me and have already started to incorporate some of the habits I wrote about. You read about something and it sparked you to action. The best time to make a new habit is when you are excited and enthusiastic. If you wait too long, your excitement will dwindle and you will forget what you were so excited about in the first place. The secret to long-term success is to try on different habits and rituals and decide which ones suit you the best and work with your lifestyle. Once you realize that MAKING it a great day and securing your happiness comes from you and you alone, that your source of happiness is renewable and you control it, you are no longer a victim to external forces, and your gain power with this knowledge. You don't have to wait until something good "happens" to you, you can MAKE something good happen to you.

Remember to be kind to yourself. As Sophia Loren said, "Mistakes are the price we pay for a full life."[1] If you never feel fear, feel foolish, make a mistake or get hurt, it means you are playing it too safe and that you need to take a chance and leave your comfort zone. When you fall down and get up again, you will experience the joy of being fully alive.

As adults, making a mistake is one of our biggest fears. We put on our perfect face for the world to see, dress in our best clothes, hop into our fabulous car, and hope nobody notices that as together as we look most of the time, we don't have it all together all the time. We don't like to make mistakes and we don't like to let on that we don't have it together. Here is where I tell you to be kind to yourself. Everyone, yes everyone, has struggles. Everyone makes mistakes from time to time. Let yourself off the hook and don't be so hard on yourself. If you make a mistake, or don't stick to a newly formed habit, lick your wounds and get up. It is all part of being human. Sometimes you are going to fall down and get a scrape and sometimes you are going to need a stretcher. That's life. The question isn't whether you are going to make mistakes or not, the question is what are you going to do when you mess up? My advice is to ask yourself some questions and perhaps journal your answers:

- What was my mistake?

- What would I do differently next time?

- What can I learn from this experience?

- How can I make myself feel better now?

If you really want to *live* in the world, you have to be willing to make some mistakes, fall down, and get your hands dirty. Take chances! Risk! Experiment! That is what this whole book is about: trying on new habits, new ideas, and new methods to see if they work for you.

You will never be the person you are capable of being if you never make any mistakes, if you never experience loneliness or fear. Your darkest moments, scariest experiences, and hardest challenges help you grow into a strong, beautiful, living soul.

I have given you tons of ideas here to copy or customize to fit your lifestyle. The bottom line is that without effort, there will be no result. If you put this book down and do nothing different, nothing will change. But I promise you if you make small changes over time and create positive habits, your whole world will change for the better.

Some people have said to me that these strategies and habits only work when you use them. They say it like it is all a bunch of garbage. I laugh and tell them that is the way it is with everything. Medicine only works when you take it.

Don't become overly concerned if you aren't changing as fast as you would like. Learning or relearning new habits happens in slow and steady increments. It is like a child learning to walk. You take a few steps and you fall down, but the next time you try you are able to a take a few more steps than you did the first time. If you stay focused on what you want, and work to keep your thoughts in alignment, your actions will follow.

You may not be able to change your life overnight, but you can change the direction tomorrow.

In the end if you take the necessary steps to create lasting positive habits, you will build a strong core and the result from that is the real you will emerge. You won't have to be one person at work and another person with your family. You will know who you are at a very deep place and you will be able to shine and be yourself without apology. You will have taken the journey into your own soul and come out stronger and more informed.

The gift is the confidence of your very being down to your core. Now you know who you are and you are no longer defined by the masses, the "sheeple" or the advertisers. You define yourself, and with this comes a strength that no one can take away from you.

> *"To be nobody but yourself in a world which is doing its best,*
> *night and day, to make you like everybody else, means to fight*
> *the hardest battle which any human being can fight; and*
> *never stop fighting."*
>
> —e. e. cummings[2]

What should you do with your core self? Start a new business, write a book, compose a song, and then change the world. Yes, that's right, take what you have learned and pass it on. Use your life as an example for others. Without even saying a word, your life will communicate passion, happiness, and wisdom. You will always know when you come across someone with a strong core, because they are never standing still and they inspire you just by living their life. You will find them teaching children to read, raising loving families, cultivating awareness for the underdog, building a skyscraper, planting a garden, or passing their knowledge on to others. They shine bright and take everyone along for the ride.

You have not just been sent here to exist. You have been sent here because you have a gift to share with the world. Don't think that this is a selfish thought. Ask yourself, what speaks to you? If it speaks to you, I guarantee you it will speak to others. Use your voice to share and pass it on.

Listen to the voice inside you. It speaks loudly and clearly to you when you stop long enough to listen to its guidance. You will be guided and you will know what to do. Find your voice. It's always been there. Use it.

Ask yourself, What do you already know in the deepest part of your being? What is your wise self saying to you? What is screaming to be acknowledged and brought to life by you? Are you living fully and completely as yourself, or are you living as a copy of someone else? The more you can be honest and genuinely who you are in every circumstance, the more the world will open up to you.

When you are comfortable in your skin, your eyes will shine, your skin will dance, and you will find extreme joy. Yesterday I was driving to the store and I passed a woman on the street who was walking her dog. She was an older woman, and had gray hair, the pretty silvery kind. I was attracted to her energy, and as I drove by her, I thought, "Wow, what a happy lady." I went on my way, finished my errands, and as I was standing in line at my local organic market, I saw this woman in line in front of me, and I thought it looked like the same woman. I asked her, "Were you just walking your dog?" "Yes," she said. I told her what I had thought as I passed her. She threw her head back, laughed, thanked me, and went on her way. Happy and fulfilled people have a light in their eyes. They have an energy that surrounds them and it is unmistakable.

Make sure you share your light with the world. Don't wait too long and we will all benefit.

Here is passage written by Marianne Williamson and one I read to myself and share with others constantly because it is so powerful.

"Our Deepest Fear"

Our deepest fear is not that we are inadequate. Our deepest fear is that we are powerful beyond measure. It is our light, not our darkness that most frightens us. We ask ourselves, Who am I to be brilliant, gorgeous, talented, fabulous? Actually, who are you not to be? You are a child of God. Your playing small does not serve the world. There is nothing enlightened about shrinking so that other people won't feel insecure around you. We are all meant to shine, as children do. We were born to make manifest the glory of God that is within us. It's not just in some of us; it's in everyone. And as we let our own light shine, we unconsciously give other people permission to do the same. As we are liberated from our own fear, our presence automatically liberates others.[3]

To get started, take my 90-Day Challenge and start creating positive, life-giving habits for yourself right now. Here is how it works:

Let me first review some of the points I made at the beginning of this book.

> **Core:** The central most important part of something. For the purpose of the challenge, your core is your mental, spiritual, emotional, and physical health.

> **Habit** A behavior pattern acquired by frequent repetition; a regular practice.

The Science Behind Habits: It takes 21 days to form a new habit, and 30 days to ensure you don't revert back to your old habit. The first three months when you are changing a habit is crucial. If you can sustain a new behavior for three months, you are less likely to relapse.

Objective: The objective of the 90-Day Challenge is to help you incorporate and develop positive habits to change your life over time. Diets, fads, depravation, and quick fixes don't work. The key to success is the development and application of simple disciplines, habits, and rituals practiced every day.

Please read through all the steps, participate at your own risk, and use good judgment. This book may offer you ideas that may or may not be good for you based on your health and fitness level. These ideas are not meant to take the place of professional advice from your doctor or therapist. Before starting any exercise or diet program, you must get medical clearance.

Step One:

- Pick ONE new habit that you would like to incorporate into your life. Pick something that will be relatively easy for you to implement for 90 days. You want to be able to focus on small victories in the beginning. If you chose something too difficult to implement and you fail too early in the process, you are more likely to give up and quit. I stress the importance of picking ONLY one habit to start. This will give you a greater chance of success.
- Write an affirmation for your new habit. For example, "I am exercising for one hour three times per week" (See Habit 12 on page 56)

- Post your new habit up in your home or office where you can see it in black and white everyday. Commit!

Step Two:

- Enlist in the support of an accountability partner: someone whom you have contact with on a regular basis. This is the person you will tell your new habit to and you will create accountability through emails, a phone call, or a weekly check-in. You will tell this person of your successes and slipups.
- If you don't have an accountability partner, create an accountability calendar. This is a calendar that you will hang up where you can see it. Yes, the old-fashioned paper kind. On the top of the month, write down the habit you are working on. At the end of each day that you stick to your habit, give yourself a gold star or something of the like. On the days you don't meet your expectations, don't do anything. No beating yourself up, no bad mouthing yourself. Be kind to yourself and start again the next day.

Step Three:

- Journal—Start a journal where you write down how you are doing with your habit. It would be ideal to write daily, even if it is only one to two sentences on how you did that day. If daily is too much, make sure to journal weekly about your progress, struggles, and the feelings you encounter. The act of journaling forces you to slow down and connect with yourself. It is impossible to journal on a regular basis without experiencing a breakthrough or gaining clarity.

Step Four:

- For the first 90 days, commit to practicing your new habit every day without fail, no matter how difficult that may be. You have to make time for this new habit to develop and become part of your routine. After 90 days, pick a new habit and add it to your first habit. Repeat for a third time after 180 days. At the end of 270 days, the goal is to have incorporated three positive, empowering habits into your life.

Examples of Habits:

Mental: I am reading ten pages every day of something that inspires, motivates, or educates me.

Physical: I am eating something green (a vegetable) every day at lunch and dinner.

Spiritual: I am spending ten minutes every day praying and/or meditating in silence.

Emotional: I am spending a total of one hour each week in positive conversation.

The key is to not rush your success and to have patience with yourself. Change and results will come over time if you take small steps. If you add one new habit every 90 days, in five years you will accumulate 20 new positive, life-inspiring habits. That's 20 new habits to help you get where you are going, versus closing this book and doing nothing different at all. You are setting your life on autopilot in the direction of your goals and dreams.

I am so thrilled you chose to take this journey with me and I wish you nothing but the best life has to offer. Please write me and let me know how you are doing at michele@key2@unlock.com.

MAKE it a great life!

Love & Light,
Michele
www.key2unlock.com

Notes

Introduction

1. MacBook Pro Dictionary Version 2.1.3 (80.4), s.v. "core."

Chapter One: Your Life Is Run by Your Habits

1. Charles Duhigg, *The Power of Habit Why We Do What We Do in Life and Business* (New York: Random House, 2012). Audiobook—stated in the beginning of the book.
2. Jim Loehr and Tony Schwartz, *The Power of Full Engagement* (New York: Free Press, 2003), 14.
3. "Twenty-One Days," *This Imperfect Journey: One Woman's Story of Recovery from Sex and Love Addiction* (blog), December 7, 2011, http://thisimperfectjourney.wordpress.com/tag/21-day-habit-theory/.
4. Mark Twain, "Habit is habit and not to be flung out the window by any man, but to be coaxed down-stairs one step at a time," *Goodreads*, accessed January 28, 2013, http://www.goodreads.com/quotes/211183-habit-is-habit-and-not-to-be-flung-out-of.
5. Martin E. P. Seligman, *Authentic Happiness: Using the New Positive Psychology to Realize Your Potential for Lasting Fulfillment* (New York: Simon & Shuster, 2002), 90–91.
6. Martin E. P. Seligman, *Learned Optimism: How to Change Your Mind and Your Life* (New York: Random House, 1991). Abridged Audio CD—source can be found early in the audiobook as it is the premise of the entire book.
7. MacBook Pro Dictionary Version 2.1.3 (80.4), s.v. "habit."

8. Loehr and Schwartz, *The Power of Full Engagement*, 7–8.

Chapter Three: Don't Ask What the World Needs . . .

1. Howard Thurman, "Don't ask what the world needs. Ask what makes you come alive, and go do it. Because what the world needs is people who have come alive," *Goodreads,* accessed November 4, 2013, http://www.goodreads.com/quotes/6273-don-t-ask-what-the-world-needs-ask-what-makes-you.
2. Jack Canfield, *Facilitation Skills Seminar* (weeklong seminar at the University of California, Santa Barbara, CA, July 1997).

Chapter Four: Cultivate Patience

1. Eckhart Tolle, in "*Stillness Speaks* by Eckhart Tolle," Oprah.com, June 9, 2008, http://www.oprah.com/oprahsbookclub/Stillness-Speaks-by-Eckhart-Tolle.
2. MacBook Pro Dictionary Version 2.1.3 (80.4), s.v. "patience."

Chapter Five: Get Enough Sleep

1. Dali Lama, "Sleep is the best medicine," *Brainy Quote*, accessed November 4, 2013, http://www.brainyquote.com/quotes/quotes/d/dalailama111631.html.
2. Dr. James Maas, "Everything You Wanted to Know about Sleep, but Were Too Tired to Ask," (presented at *One Day University* at the NY Hilton, October 24, 2013).

Chapter Six: Visualize Your Tomorrow Tonight

1. Dr. Wayne Dyer. *Wishes Fulfilled* (Carlsbad, Hay House, 2012). Audiobook—referenced in the beginning of the audio and during the 5th Wishes fulfilled Foundation.
2. Michael Phelps, in Anthony Fernando, "Michael Phelps—5 Secrets of Success," August 18, 2008, http://www.anthonyfernando.com/2008/08/18/michael-phelps-five-secrets-of-success/.

Chapter Seven: Inspire, Motivate, or Educate Yourself in the Morning

1. Jim Rohn, "Formal education will earn you a living; self-education will earn you a fortune," *Brainy Quote*, accessed November 4, 2013, http://www.brainyquote.com/quotes/quotes/j/jimrohn121282.html.

Chapter Eight: Eat Breakfast

1. Geneen Roth, *Women Food and God: An Unexpected Path to Almost Everything* (New York: Scribner, 2010), cover flaps. Web. http://www.amazon.com/Women-Food-God-Unexpected-Everything/dp/1416543082/ref=sr_sp-atf_title_1_1?s=books&ie=UTF8&qid=1383598021&sr=1-1&keywords=god+women+and+food.
2. Michael Pollan, *Food Rules* (New York, Penguin Books, 2009), 43.
3. Jeanie Lerche Davis, "Lose Weight, Eat Breakfast," *WebMD*, accessed November 4, 2103, http://www.webmd.com/diet/features/lose-weight-eat-breakfast.

Chapter Nine: Juice When You Can

1. Jack LaLanne, "LaLanneisms," *Jack LaLanne*, BeFit Enterprises, accessed November 4, 2013, http://www.jacklalanne.com/jacks-adventures/lalanneisms.php.
2. "Feats and Honors," *Jack LaLanne*, BeFit Enterprises, accessed March 19, 2013, http://www.jacklalanne.com/jacks-adventures/feats-and-honors.php.

Chapter Ten: Eliminate What Is Not Working

1. Timothy Ferriss, *The 4-Hour Work Week: Escape 9–5, Live Anywhere, and Join the New Rich* (New York, Crown Publishers, 2007), 109.

Chapter Eleven: Move Your Body Every Day

1. "Those who think they don't have time for bodily exercise, will sooner or later have to find time for illness," Edward Stanely, *ExRx.net*, November 4, 2013, http://www.exrx.net/ExInfo/Quotes.html.
2. Gabrielle Reece, In an article on her years ago, she made similar remarks in her article, "6 Simple Tips to Get in Shape,"

MindBodyGreen, March 16, 2012, http://www.mindbodygreen.com/0-4265/6-Simple-Tips-to-Get-in-Shape.html.

3. Sonja Lyubomirsky, *The How of Happiness: A New Approach to Getting the Life You Want* (New York: Penguin, 2007), 244.

Chapter Twelve: Listen to Audiobooks in the Shower

1. Juvenal, "All wish to possess knowledge, but few, comparatively speaking, are willing to pay the price," *Brainy Quote*, November 4, 2013, http://www.brainyquote.com/quotes/quotes/j/juvenal122569.html.

Chapter Thirteen: Guide Your Thoughts All Day Long

1. Henry David Thoreau, "As a single footstep will not make a path on the earth, so a single thought will not make a pathway in the mind. To make a deep physical path, we walk again and again. To make a deep mental path, we must think over and over the kind of thoughts we wish to dominate our lives," *Goodreads*, November 4, 2013, http://www.goodreads.com/quotes/tag/power-of-thoughts.

2. Brian Tracy, "Understanding your Conscious Mind," Brian Tracy International (blog), November 2, 2010, http://www.briantracy.com/blog/general/understanding-your-conscious-mind/.

3. Jack Canfield, *The Success Principles* (New York: Harper Collins, 2005), 229.

4. Brian Tracy, "Understanding your Concious Mind," Brian Tracy International (blog), November 2, 2010, http://www.briantracy.com/blog/general/understanding-your-conscious-mind/.

5. George Dvorsky, "Managing Your 50,000 Daily Thoughts," *Sentient Developments* (blog), March 19, 2007, http://www.sentientdevelopments.com/2007/03/managing-your-50000-daily-thoughts.html.

6. Jill Bolte Taylor, *My Stroke of Insight: A Brain Scientist's Personal Journey* (New York: Penguin, 2008), 32, 33, 35, 44, 45, 110, 111,123, 124.

7. Bruce Lipton, *The Biology of Belief* (Carlsbad, CA: Hay House, 2008). Audiobook—referenced midway through the audiobook, (author also took notes in her personal journal #11 in February 2011).

Chapter Fourteen: Have a Clear Vision and Goals

1. Marjorie Blanchard, author of *One Minute Manager*, quoted in "Target Your Dream Job," *Vitali Training & Coaching* http://www8. georgetown.edu/advancement/alumni/careerservices/slides/Dream_ Job_Webinar_1_7_10.pdf.
2. Jack Canfield, *Facilitation Skills Seminar* (weeklong seminar at the University of California, Santa Barbara, CA, July 1997).
3. Daniel Pink, *DRIVE: The Surprising Truth about What Motivates Us* (New York: Riverhead Books, 2009). Audiobook—referenced in chapter 5, (author took notes in her personal journal #9 February 2010).
4. Ibid.
5. Ibid.
6. Dan Buettner, *The Blue Zones: 9 Lessons for Living Longer* (Washington DC: National Geographic Society, 2008). Audiobook, (author took notes in her personal journal #13, July 2011, Lesson Five: Purpose Now).
7. Martin E. P. Seligman, *Authentic Happiness: Using the New Positive Psychology to Realize Your Potential for Lasting Fulfillment* (New York: Simon & Shuster, 2002), 249.
8. Canfield, *Facilitation Skills Seminar*.

Chapter Fifteen: Create Affirmations for Your Goals and Dreams

1. Alfred Montapert, "To accomplish great things, we must first dream, then visualize, then plan . . . believe . . . act," *Brainy Quote*, November 4, 2013, http://www.brainyquote.com/quotes/quotes/a/ alfredamo166039.html.
2. Bruce Lipton, *The Biology of Belief* (Carlsbad, CA: Hay House, 2008). Audiobook—referenced in the beginning, (author took notes in her personal journal #11 in February 2011).
3. Ibid.
4. Jack Canfield, *Facilitation Skills Seminar* (weeklong seminar at the University of California, Santa Barbara, CA, July 1997).

Chapter Sixteen: Create Visual Affirmations, Posters, and Reminders

1. Jack Welch, "Good business leaders create a vision, articulate the vision, passionately own the vision, and relentlessly drive it to completion,"

Thinkexist.com, accessed November 4, 2013, http://thinkexist.com/
quotation/good_business_leaders_create_a_vision-articulate/151585.
html.

2. "Mere-exposure effect," *Wikipedia*, last modified October 22, 2013,
http://en.wikipedia.org/wiki/Mere-exposure_effect.

Chapter Seventeen: Start a Mastermind Group

1. Napoleon Hill, *Think and Grow Rich* (New York: Tribeca Books,
1937), 168–69.

Chapter Eighteen: Be Grateful and Celebrate Your Wins

1. Oprah Winfrey, "The more you praise and celebrate your life, the
more there is in life to celebrate," *Thinkexist.com*, accessed November
4, 2013, http://thinkexist.com/quotation/the_more_you_praise_and_
celebrate_your_life-the/217679.html.

2. Sonja Lyubomirsky, *The How of Happiness: A New Approach to Getting
the Life You Want* (New York: Penguin, 2007), 90.

Chapter Nineteen: Let Life Touch You

1. Travis Bradberry and Jean Graves, *The Emotional Intelligence Quick
Book* (New York: Fireside, 2003), 39.

2. The Free Dictionary, by Farlex, s.v. "inspire," November 8, 2013, http://
www.thefreedictionary.com/inspire.

Chapter Twenty: Pay Attention to the NOW

1. Will Rogers, "Don't let yesterday take up too much of today,"
Goodreads, November 4, 2013, http://www.goodreads.com/
quotes/47409-don-t-let-yesterday-take-up-too-much-of-today.

2. Richard Wiseman, *The Luck Factor* (New York: Hyperion, 2004), 45, 54.

Chapter Twenty-One: Only Let into Your Life the Things You Want to Influence You

1. Brian L. Crissey, "Granite Publishing, LLC Manuscript Submission
Guidelines," accessed February 5, 2013, http://www.granitepublishing.
us/root/SubmissionGuidelines.html.

Chapter Twenty-Two: Motivate with Music

1. Berthold Auerbach, "Music washes away from the soul the dust of everyday life," *Quotations Book*, http://quotationsbook.com/ quote/27572/#sthash.CT1HM2US.dpbs.
2. "Using Music to Change Your Mood," 2 Know Myself, updated November 4, 2013, http://www.2knowmyself.com/Music_therapy/ changing_your_mood_using_music_stress.
3. Ibid.

Chapter Twenty-Three: Spend Time in Self-Reflection

1. Hans Margolius, "Only in quiet waters things mirror themselves. Only in a quiet mind is adequate perception of the world," *Quotations Book*, accessed November 4, 2013, http://quotationsbook.com/ quote/29817/#sthash.SFkK543B.dpbs.
2. Stephen Covey, *The Seven Habits of Successful People Workshop* (New York City, NY).
3. Daniel Pink, *A Whole New Mind: Why Right-Brainers Will Rule the Future* (New York: Riverhead, 2005). Audiobook—near the beginning of the audio, (author took notes in her personal journal #5 in November 2008).

Chapter Twenty-Four: Journal

1. Christina Baldwin, "Journal writing is a voyage to the interior," *Thinkexist.com*, accessed November 4, 2013, http://thinkexist.com/ quotation/journal_writing_is_a_voyage_to_the/255087.html.
2. Michael Gelb, *How to think Like Leonardo da Vinci: Seven Steps to Genius Every Day* (New York: Delacorte Press, 1998), 57.
3. Sonja Lyubomirsky, *The How of Happiness: A New Approach to Getting the Life You Want* (New York: Penguin, 2007), 163–65.

Chapter Twenty-Five: Take Responsibility for Your Reactions

1. Victor E. Frankl, "When we are no longer able to change the situation, we are challenged to change ourselves," *Brainy Quote*, accessed November 5, 2013, http://www.brainyquote.com/quotes/quotes/v/ viktorefr121087.html.

2. Travis Bradberry and Jean Graves, *The Emotional Intelligence Quick Book* (New York: Fireside, 2003), 121.
3. Jack Canfield, *The Success Principles* (New York: Harper Collins, 2005), 3, 6, 7.

Chapter Twenty-Six: Become an Optimist

1. Hugh Downs, "A happy person is not a person with a certain set of circumstances, but rather a person with a certain set of attitudes," in "What Is Happiness? Top 10 Quotes," *Great Quotes on Life*, accessed November 5, 2013, http://www.great-quotes-on-life.com/what-is-happiness.html.
2. "Positive Psychology," *Wikipedia*, last modified November 3, 2013, http://en.wikipedia.org/wiki/Positive_psychology.
3. Martin E. P. Seligman, *Learned Optimism: How to Change Your Mind and Your Life* (New York: Random House, 1991). Abridged Audio CD. See also Martin E. P. Seligman, *Authentic Happiness: Using the New Positive Psychology to Realize Your Potential for Lasting Fulfillment* (New York: Simon & Shuster, 2002), 24.
4. Ibid.
5. Sonja Lyubomirsky, *The How of Happiness: A New Approach to Getting the Life You Want* (New York: Penguin, 2007), 20–23.
6. Ibid.
7. Martin E. P. Seligman, *Authentic Happiness: Using the New Positive Psychology to Realize Your Potential for Lasting Fulfillment* (New York: Simon & Shuster, 2002), 49.
8. Lyubomirsky, *The How of Happiness*, 14.
9. Winston Churchill, "A pessimist sees the difficulty in every opportunity; an optimist sees the opportunity in every difficulty," *Thinkexist.com*, accessed November 5, 2013, http://thinkexist.com/quotation/a_pessimist_sees_the_difficulty_in_every/15269.html.
10. Seligman, *Authentic Happiness*, 88–91, 226.

Chapter Twenty-Seven: If You Are Living, Be Learning

1. Richard Bach, "Here is a test to find whether your mission on earth is finished. If you're alive, it isn't," *Thinkexist.com*, accessed November 5, 2013, http://thinkexist.com/quotation/here_is_the_test_to_find_whether_your_mission_on/8259.html.

2.   Tony Hsieh, *Delivering Happiness: A Path to Profits, Passion, and Purpose* (New York: Hachette Book Group, 2010), 165.

Chapter Twenty-Eight: Go Outside

1.   Henry David Thoreau, "An early morning walk is a blessing for the whole day," *Brainy Quote*, accessed November 5, 2013, http://www.brainyquote.com/quotes/quotes/h/henrydavid108393.html.
2.   Sonja Lyubomirsky, *The How of Happiness: A New Approach to Getting the Life You Want* (New York: Penguin, 2007), 197.

Chapter Twenty-Nine: Give Smiles

1.   George Carlin, "Everyone smiles in the same language," *Goodreads*, accessed November 5, 2013, http://www.goodreads.com/quotes/272414-everyone-smiles-in-the-same-language.
2.   Charlie Pulsipher, "15 Health Benefits of Smiling," *Sunwarrior*, April 17, 2013, http://www.sunwarrior.com/news/15-health-benefits-of-smiling/.

Chapter Thirty: Eat from the Earth

1.   Michael Pollan, *Food Rules* (New York: Penguin Books, 2009), 7.
2.   Ibid., xii.

Chapter Thirty-One: Connect with Your Spiritual Side

1.   Wayne Dyer, quoting Joel Goldsmith, forward to *Left to Tell*, by Immaculée Ilibagiza and Steve Erwin (Carlsbad, CA: Hay House, 2006). See also Wayne Dyer, "Immaculée Ilibagiza, Author of Left To Tell," Dr. Wayne W. Dyer, accessed November 5, 2013, http://www.drwaynedyer.com/articles/immaculee-ilibagiza-author-of-left-to-tell.
2.   Daniel Pink, *A Whole New Mind: Why Right-Brainers Will Rule the Future* (New York: Riverhead, 2005). Audiobook—toward the end of the audio, (author took notes on this in her personal journal #5 in January 2009).
3.   Martin E. P. Seligman, *Authentic Happiness: Using the New Positive Psychology to Realize Your Potential for Lasting Fulfillment* (New York: Simon & Shuster, 2002), 249.

4. Sonja Lyubomirsky, *The How of Happiness: A New Approach to Getting the Life You Want* (New York: Penguin, 2007), 228–32.
5. Dan Buettner, *The Blue Zones: 9 Lessons for Living Longer* (Washington DC: National Geographic Society, 2008). Audiobook.

Chapter Thirty-Two: Unplug

1. Stephen Covey, *FOCUS: Achieving Your Highest Priorities Workbook* (FranklinCovey, 2002), 28.
2. Suzy Graves and Lauren Hadden, ed. "You Just Keep Me Hanging On . . .," *Psychologies Magazine*. October 2013, 85.

Chapter Thirty-Three: Nurture Relationships

1. Trevor Stokes Reuters, as quoted in Jeanna Bryner, "You gotta have friends? Most have just 2 true pals," *LiveScience*, on NBC News Health, November 4, 2011, http://vitals.nbcnews.com/_news/2011/11/04/8637894-you-gotta-have-friends-most-have-just-2-true-pals.
2. Eleanor Roosevelt, "Great minds discuss ideas, average minds discuss events, and small minds discuss people," *Brainy Quote*, accessed November 5, 2013, http://www.brainyquote.com/quotes/quotes/e/eleanorroo385439.html.

Chapter Thirty-Four: Have a Bad-Day Emergency Plan

1. Richard Kline, "Confidence is preparation. Everything else is beyond your control," *Thinkexist.com*, accessed November 5, 2013, http://thinkexist.com/quotation/confidence_is_preparation-everything_else_is/224487.html.
2. Travis Bradberry and Jean Graves, *The Emotional Intelligence Quick Book* (New York: Fireside, 2003), 121.
3. Jill Bolte Taylor, *My Stroke of Insight: A Brain Scientist's Personal Journey* (New York: Penguin, 2008), 146.
4. Eleanor Rosevelt, "No one can make you feel inferior without your consent," *Goodreads*, accessed November 5, 2013, http://www.goodreads.com/quotes/11035-no-one-can-make-you-feel-inferior-without-your-consent.
5. Albert Camus, "A friend is someone who knows the song in your heart and can sing it back to you when you have forgotten the words," *Search*

Quotes, accessed November 5, 2013, http://www.searchquotes.com/quotation/A_friend_is_someone_who_knows_the_song_in_your_heart_and_can_sing_it_back_to_you_when_you_have_forgo/509/.

Chapter Thirty-Five: Use Your God-Given Talents as Much as Possible

1. Erma Bombeck, "When I stand before God at the end of my life, I would hope that I would not have a single bit of talent left, and I could say, 'I used everything you gave me,'" *Brainy Quote*, accessed November 5, 2013, http://www.brainyquote.com/quotes/quotes/e/ermabombec106409.html.

Chapter Thirty-Six: Do Something Kind

1. Annie Lennox, "Ask yourself: Have you been kind today? Make kindness your daily modus operandi and change your world," *Brainy Quote*, accessed November 5, 2013, http://www.brainyquote.com/quotes/quotes/a/annielenno390787.html.

Chapter Thirty-Seven: Love People, Engage Them and Connect

1. Bishop Desmond Tutu, "My humanity is bound up in yours, for we can only be human together," *Brainy Quote*, accessed November 5, 2013, http://www.brainyquote.com/quotes/quotes/d/desmondtut383784.html.
2. Dale Carnegie, *How To Win Friends and Influence People* (New York: Simon & Schuster, 1936), 64.
3. Maya Angelou, interview by Oprah Winfrey, *Oprah Winfrey Show*, King World Productions and CBS Television Distribution, 1986–2011.
4. "Connect with Others: How Connections Help," reviewed by Sonja Lyubomirsky, *Live your Life Well*, from Mental Health America, accessed November 5, 2013, http://www.liveyourlifewell.org/go/live-your-life-well/connect.
5. Roko Belic, *Happy*, directed by Roko Belic, 2011. Wadi Rum Films, 2012. DVD, 75 min.

Chapter Thirty-Eight: Be Flexible to Become Strong

1. Anthony Lawlor, "Thus, flexibility, as displayed by water, is a sign of life. Rigidity, its opposite, is an indicator of death," *Search Quotes*,

accessed November 5, 2013, http://www.searchquotes.com/quotation/
Thus,_flexibility,_as_displayed_by_water,_is_a_sign_of_life._
Rigidity,_its_opposite,_is_an_indicator/414759/.

2. MacBook Pro Dictionary Version 2.1.3 (80.4), s.v. "strong."
3. The Boston Transcript, William Jay Poem, *Quotes, Ideas and Advice* (blog), September 26, 2011, http://quoteideaadvice.blogspot.com/2011/09/here-lies-body-of-william-jay-who-died.html.

Chapter Thirty-Nine: Take Responsibility for Your Energy

1. Jill Bolte Taylor, *My Stroke of Insight: A Brain Scientist's Personal Journey* (New York: Penguin, 2008), 120.

Chapter Forty: Nourish Your Passion

1. Georg Wilhelm Friedrich Hegel, "Nothing great in the world has been accomplished without passion," *Brainy Quote*, accessed November 5, 2013, http://www.brainyquote.com/quotes/quotes/g/georgwilhe101479.html.
2. MacBook Pro Dictionary Version 2.1.3 (80.4), s.v. "passion."
3. The Free Dictionary, by Farlex, s.v. "enthusiasim," November 5, 2013, http://www.thefreedictionary.com/enthusiasm.
4. Norman Vincent Peale, "Throw your heart over the fence and the rest will follow," *The Quotations Page*, accessed November 5, 2013, http://www.quotationspage.com/quote/2527.html.

Chapter Forty-One: Say Yes to Adventure and Leave Your Comfort Zone

1. E. B. White, "I arise in the morning torn between the desire to improve the world and a desire to enjoy the world. This makes it hard to plan the day," *Brainy Quote*, accessed November 5, 2013, http://www.brainyquote.com/quotes/quotes/e/ebwhite106410.html.

Chapter Forty-Three: Drink Water

1. Leonardo da Vinci, "Water is the driving force of all nature," *Brainy Quote*, November 5, 2013, http://www.brainyquote.com/quotes/quotes/l/leonardoda151978.html.

2. Bill Phillips, Adam Campbell, Kevin Donahue, Dan Revitte, Trevor Thieme, Mike Darling, Chris Rackliffe, et al., "15 Easy Ways to Speed Up Your Metabolism," *Men's Health*, on *Active*, accessed November 5, 2013, http://www.active.com/fitness/articles/15-easy-ways-to-speed-up-your-metabolism.

Chapter Forty-Four: Know How to Find Your Center

1. Lao Tzu, "At the center of your being you have the answer; you know who you are and you know what you want," *Brainy Quote*, accessed November 5, 2013, http://www.brainyquote.com/quotes/quotes/l/laotzu386562.html.
2. Bruce Lipton, *The Biology of Belief* (Carlsbad, CA: Hay House, 2008). Audiobook, (author took notes on this in her personal journal #11 in February 2011).

Chapter Forty-Five: Use Your Words Wisely

1. "If someone were to pay you 10 cents for every kind word you ever spoke and collect from you 5 cents for every unkind word, would you be rich or poor," blog post, http://thejourneybegins.edublogs.org/ms-aherns-posts/the-power-of-words/.

Chapter Forty-Six: Make Time to Play

1. Ralph Waldo Emerson, "We are always getting ready to live, but never living," *Brainy Quote*, accessed November 5, 2013, http://www.brainyquote.com/quotes/quotes/r/ralphwaldo104462.html.
2. Sonja Lyubomirsky, *The How of Happiness: A New Approach to Getting the Life You Want* (New York: Penguin, 2007), 190–91.

Chapter Forty-Seven: Create Relationship Rituals

1. Guillaume Musso, "As long as you remember the person who loved you, and whom you still love, then you're making love endure," *Goodreads*, http://www.goodreads.com/quotes/686463-as-long-as-you-remember-the-person-who-loved-you.

Conclusion

1. Sophia Loren, "Mistakes are the price we pay for a full life," *43 Things*, http://www.43things.com/entries/view/5846584.
2. e. e. cummings, "To be nobody but yourself, in a world which is doing its best, night and day, to make you like everybody else, means to fight the hardest battle which any human being can fight; and never stop fighting," *Brainy Quote*, accessed November 5, 2013, http://www.brainyquote.com/quotes/authors/e/e_e_cummings.html.
3. Marianne Williamson, *A Return To Love: Reflections on the Principles of A Course in Miracles*, (New York: HarperCollins, 1992), 190–91. See also http://skdesigns.com/internet/articles/quotes/williamson/our_deepest_fear/

About the Author

Michele Phillips has had a zest for living life full out since she was a child. Inspired by her dad who always had her singing and dancing around the house, Michele unconsciously developed happy habits.

As the president of Key Performance (www.key2unlock.com), Michele has been on a lifelong quest to help others create positive habits that build confidence, increase vitality, and help people move in the direction of their goals and dreams. Michele's professional experience spans over 20 years facilitating engaging workshops, seminars, and coaching programs with Fortune 500 companies around the globe including, TAG Heuer, Pfizer Pharmaceuticals, Barclay's Capital, Verizon Wireless, and COACH leather, just to name a few. An authority in the field of peak performance, Michele inspires others to action and helps individuals create lives filled with energy, joy, and positive habits.

Michele is happily married and lives in the Hudson Valley right outside New York City, but her love of travel makes it hard for her to stay home for long, so she likes to think of herself as a citizen of the world.

To stay up to date with Michele, find out where she is speaking next, attend a public workshop, book Michele to speak, or receive her blog, please subscribe at www.key2unlock.com.